LEADOCRACY

This special book is
signed by the author
Geoff Smart.

D1011088

PRAISE FOR *LEADOCRACY*

Entrepreneurs

"*Leadocracy* is a refreshingly simply solution to the problem of government dysfunction." —H. Wayne Huizenga, Chairman, Huizenga Holdings and former Founder and CEO of three Fortune 500 companies

"At a time of deep doubt about the ability of our federal government to manage our country, *Leadocracy* provides a reason for hope. As Geoff Smart demonstrates in this timely book, with great leadership no problem is unsolvable." —Ken Griffin, CEO of Citadel

"As someone who has seen up close hundreds of companies succeed or fail, I can tell you that the quality of the leader is the number one driver of success. *Leadocracy* shows how to get more great leaders into government, which we sorely need." —Steve Schwarzman, Chairman, CEO, and Cofounder, The Blackstone Group

"If we don't have leadership in this country with the experience to develop a smart long-term economic growth plan, the guts to aggressively execute it, and the perseverance to stick with it over the long haul, we'll never again see the economic prosperity we've come to take for granted." —Ted Waitt, Chairman, Avalon Capital Group and Waitt Family Foundation, Founder & former CEO of Gateway

"Leadership is the key to human progress. Geoff Smart's book leads the way." —Charles Butt, Chairman, H-E-B

"If we can systematically find ways to attract our best leaders to government, as *Leadocracy* describes, the quality of life of our society will improve." —John Malone, Ph.D., Chairman, Liberty Media Corporation

Government Leaders

"Our future, the world's future, depends on attracting better leaders to government. *Leadocracy* provides a blueprint for how to do it. Reading it is an inspiration." —Governor John W. Hickenlooper of Colorado

"*Leadocracy* documents what we in Indiana have learned firsthand: With leadership from citizens possessing the right mix of experience and vision, good government is not a lost cause." —Governor Mitch Daniels of Indiana

"Geoff Smart makes clear the compelling need for top talent to choose public service. *Leadocracy* demonstrates the difference strong leadership makes in the public and private sectors." —Governor Jack Markell of Delaware

"Private sector leadership is badly needed in the public sector. *Leadocracy* shows us how to make this happen." —Mark Emkes, Commissioner of Finance & Administration, State of Tennessee, and former CEO of Bridgestone Americas

"It is high time that we focus far more on improving the return on investment of our tax dollars. The best approach for accomplishing this is for successful business leaders to step forward and give back by applying their wealth of practical business experience and objective fact-based analysis to government leadership and decision making." —Fred Steingraber, President of Kenilworth, IL, and Chairman Emeritus, A.T. Kearney

"Nothing we do in government is as important as who we hire into key leadership roles. *Leadocracy*, and Geoff's previous book *Who*, outline principles that we have applied with great success here in Colorado." —Roxane White, Chief of Staff to Governor John Hickenlooper of Colorado

"What a 'Smart' book! *Leadocracy* redefines government leadership and what it should be, results-based and focused on why true leaders choose to work in government—to help better the lives of others in a streamlined, efficient, and accountable manner." —Lynn Johnson, Executive Director, Jefferson County, CO, Department of Human Services

"I was in business, then served as Mayor of Warrenton, Virginia where we improved government services, slashed taxes 75 percent, and led the country with our Green Initiative. *Leadocracy* is not fiction, it is real!" —George Fitch, former Mayor of Warrenton, VA

"The problems of government are not insurmountable, if the right leaders are in charge. *Leadocracy* is our way forward." —Mayor Charles Harris of York, NE

Social Entrepreneurs

"Education reform and government reform are inter-related. I believe that leadership is the answer to both. I applaud Geoff Smart's initiative and willingness to bring his hiring methods into the public sector with *Leadocracy*." —Wendy Kopp, Founder, Teach For America

"Looking for a silver bullet solution to the world's problems? It isn't money, technology, or a magical pill. I'm with Geoff; it's leadership." —Nancy Lublin, CEO and Chief Old Person, dosomething.org

"As *Leadocracy* points out, whether you are in the social or private sector, leadership is about releasing the energy in others." —Robin Wise, President & CEO, Junior Achievement–Rocky Mountain

"We have used Geoff Smart's methods for hiring here at KIPP with great results. We would love to see them applied to how government leaders are selected, the way he outlines in *Who* and *Leadocracy*." —Mike Feinberg and David Levin, Cofounders, KIPP (Knowledge is Power Program, the largest charter school operator in the United States)

Leading Scholars

"A high-performing government requires high-performing leaders; *Leadocracy* convincingly shows that we have an under-tapped supply in the private sector and desperately need to engage them." —Professor Steven Kaplan of The University of Chicago Booth School of Business

"I am encouraged by the idea of more great private sector leaders going into the public sector, a trend which *Leadocracy* outlines." —Professor Morten Sorensen, Columbia Business School

"The evaluation of any organization starts with an assessment of the leader. Geoff Smart has made a compelling case for leader-oriented government reform in *Leadocracy*." —Professor Stewart Donaldson, Dean & Chair of Psychology, Claremont Graduate University

"Part diagnosis, part call-to-arms, Geoff Smart's *Leadocracy* injects a thought-provoking new voice into the dialogue about how to improve our government. It will hopefully spark better leaders to seek key positions at all levels of government." —Professor Noam Wasserman, Harvard Business School, author of *The Founder's Dilemmas: Anticipating and Avoiding the Pitfalls That Can Sink a Startup*

Bestselling Authors

"Geoff Smart is the world expert on the topic of hiring leaders. What he suggests we do in *Leadocracy* to get more great leaders into government is wise counsel." —Marshall Goldsmith, the world's #1 Leadership Thinker (Thinkers50, *Harvard Business Review*) and *New York Times* bestselling author or editor of 31 books, including *What Got You Here Won't Get You There*

"Geoff Smart is one of the nation's top thinkers on how to hire great people. And he has put his finger on our fundamental failure as voters—we don't hire great people into government. *Leadocracy* shows how that can change." —Atul Gawande, MD, surgeon and bestselling author of *The Checklist Manifesto*

CEOs

"*Leadocracy* helps to demystify government, and shows how great leaders from the private sector can make a difference in the public sector, for the good of us all." —Aaron Kennedy, Founder, Noodles & Company

"Geoff Smart's previous book, *Who*, was the number one most impactful book on my career as a CEO. I am hopeful *Leadocracy* will be as impactful on society." —Craig Zoberis, CEO, Fusion OEM

"It is about time this subject got the thoughtful treatment it deserves. The sad fact is our government is a source of competitive disadvantage for our country. The happy fact is Geoff's book may start to change that." —Kent Thiry, Chairman & CEO, DaVita

"I would LOVE to see more of Geoff Smart's principles of hiring applied to how we choose our government leaders." —Kevin Burns, Managing Principal, Lazard Technology Partners, and former CEO of InterSolv

"Geoff is an absolute wonder to work with, and even more so to experience! His brilliantly simple approach to the seemingly complex issues of leadership is second to none." —Leslie Baum, Senior Director of Global Learning, Entrepreneurs' Organization, and Director of EO's Entrepreneurial Masters Program

"The world continues to grow in complexity while the democratic process we use to govern has become mired in bureaucracy and increasingly ineffective. *Leadocracy* offers a provocative new strategy to engage our strongest leaders, enabling government agencies to deliver more with less." —Mark Hopkins, Managing Partner, Cresendo Capital Partners, Former CEO of Peak Industries, and author of *Shortcut to Prosperity*

"One of my main goals in business is to find and grow great leaders. Our success depends on it. Sadly, there is no such training ground in government. We should expect more from our politicians and *Leadocracy* makes a strong case for greater private participation in the public sector." —Mike Fries, CEO, Liberty Global

"*Leadocracy* provides practical and thoughtful suggestions on how to attract great leaders into government." —Mark T. Gallogly, Managing Principal and Cofounder, Centerbridge Partners

"Geoff Smart's methods have helped me hire a great team. I can only imagine how much good will be done for society when this approach is applied to hiring government leaders." —Scott Clawson, President, GSI

"Great leaders go through stages in their careers. *Leadocracy* makes a great case for why one of those stages should be a stint in government." —Chrismon Nofsinger, Ph.D., CEO, The Nofsinger Group, and author of *The Shift From One to Many*

"Geoff Smart is 'the man' when it comes to hiring. I am pleased to see him applying his methods to the daunting task of selecting government leaders. *Leadocracy* is a step in the right direction." —Darrin Anderson, RVP, HD Supply

"I loved my job in the private sector. I love my job in the public sector. People seem to think that government is only about gridlock and dysfunction. It's not, as *Leadocracy* illustrates. Great leaders can make a huge difference, and they can have a fun and meaningful chapter of their career in government."—Ken Lund, Executive Director, Office of Economic Development and International Trade, and former Managing Partner, HRO

"I used to say that I would never in a million years consider going into government. However, *Leadocracy* has changed my mind." —Greg Alexander, CEO, Sales Benchmark Index, and author of *Making the Number*

"Geoff Smart's approach to hiring was game changing for me as CEO, which allowed my team to deliver a 67 percent internal rate of return to our investors. I can only hope his expertise has the same kind of impact on the world of government leadership, which badly needs it." —Panos Anastassiadis, former CEO of Cyveillence

"Finding a way to get more ethical and competent leaders in government is critical for the future of our way of life. *Leadocracy* applies Geoff Smart's hiring method to the public sector, which badly needs it." —Selim Bassoul, Chairman & CEO, Middleby Corporation

"*Leadocracy* is bound to be one of the most impactful books of our generation. Government desperately needs more great leaders. Great leaders need a sense of meaning and challenge in their careers. When the two come together, the game will change for the better." —Eric Cohen, President, Power Plant Services

"I have limited time and choose the business books I read carefully. They must be logical but simple, compelling but fun, and above all direct us on how to make an impact. Once again Geoff has inspired me." —Paul Ford, CEO, Total Attorneys

"*Leadocracy* signals a movement that is underway to hire more great leaders into government. I hope my fellow Brits figure this one out too; our way of life depends on it." —Richard Bryan, Managing Director, BBH Properties

"Thousands of successful entrepreneurs around the world know about Geoff Smart's ideas about leadership and performance, and they apply them with great success. In *Leadocracy*, I am pleased to see the world of government is starting to take note." —Verne Harnish, Founder, Entrepreneurs' Organization, and author of *Mastering the Rockefeller Habits*

LEADOCRACY

HIRING MORE GREAT LEADERS (LIKE YOU)
INTO GOVERNMENT

GEOFF SMART

COAUTHOR OF THE *NEW YORK TIMES* BESTSELLER *WHO*

GREENLEAF
BOOK GROUP PRESS

Published by Greenleaf Book Group Press
Austin, Texas
www.gbgpress.com

Distributed by Greenleaf Book Group LLC

For ordering information or special discounts for bulk purchases, please contact Greenleaf Book Group LLC at PO Box 91869, Austin, TX 78709, 512.891.6100.

Design and composition by Greenleaf Book Group LLC
Cover design by Greenleaf Book Group LLC

Publisher's Cataloging-In-Publication Data
(Prepared by The Donohue Group, Inc.)
Smart, Geoff.
    Leadocracy : hiring more great leaders (like you) into government / Geoff Smart.—1st ed.
        p. : ill., charts ; cm.
    The first "a" in "Leadocracy" in title is underlined.
    ISBN: 978-1-60832-288-6
    1. Bureaucracy. 2. Leadership. 3. Government employees—Recruiting. 4. Employee selection. I. Title.
JF1501 .S62 2012
351   2011945634

Part of the Tree Neutral® program, which offsets the number of trees consumed in the production and printing of this book by taking proactive steps, such as planting trees in direct proportion to the number of trees used: www.treeneutral.com

TreeNeutral®

Printed in the United States of America on acid-free paper

12 13 14 15 16 17   10 9 8 7 6 5 4 3 2 1

First Edition

Contents

This book is dedicated to my father, Brad Smart.
Thanks, Pop, for the lively dinner-table debates
about society's problems and solutions.

Solving Our #1 Problem

"Life just gets better and better."

Virgil Johnson was fond of this saying. He repeated it to his family again and again over the years. And when he said it, he said it with a smile. Because he meant it. It was true for him.

I remember the day that Dr. Johnson met my newborn son, Will, for the first time. Virgil was my wife's grandfather. He smiled with pride, and held Will high up in the air and told him, "Life just gets better and better." It didn't mean much to our wide-eyed boy at the time, but it left an impression on me. Later that day, the old man passed away.

That was ten years ago, a time when terrorism was on the rise, countries were becoming unstable, government spending ran rampant, the economy was uncertain at best.

Since then, the situation has gotten worse.

When I heard the news of Virgil's passing, a question crept into my mind. It was a question that I tried to ignore for years. But about eighteen months ago, I was forced to face it.

Will life get better and better?

I was not sure of the answer. Like many of you who are reading this book, I was cynical about the state of our country and about our leaders' ability to improve it. And I wasn't alone in my opinions. In June 2011, Gallup polled adults from across the United States. Forty-eight percent of those polled indicated that they had very little or no confidence in the U.S. Congress. Of the sixteen institutions listed, including the criminal justice system, labor unions, banks, and HMOs, the U.S. Congress ranked lowest in confidence.[1] Only 12 percent of people said that they had a great deal or quite a lot of confidence in our Congress, and that number has been on a downward trend ever since 1973, when the poll was first taken.

But in December of 2010, I got an email that changed my life, and may change yours.

It was a request to help my state's newly elected governor, John Hickenlooper, select his cabinet. This email would start me off on an unexpected journey, an exploration of the realities of leadership in government.

What I discovered shocked me.

I began the journey expecting to find nothing but gridlock, corruption, and dysfunction in government. I was prepared to confirm my worst fear, that society as we know it is doomed.

During this journey, I got to see for myself what government was all about. I was able to talk candidly with, and in some cases work alongside, leaders who had taken the big leap from the private sector into government. Do you want to know what I found?

Society is not doomed after all.

Government, though highly dysfunctional today, is not a problem without a solution.

If you are rubbing your eyes in disbelief at what you just read, this book is for you. If you care about your own career happiness and your own life getting better and better, this book is for you. If you care about the lives of your friends and family and their kids' lives getting better and better, this book is for you.

Thank you for joining me on this journey. If this book changes your mind, please help me spread the word. Give this book as a gift. Talk it up. Help to accelerate movement in the right direction to solve our number one problem.

Our #1 Problem

What do we need in order to enjoy a life that gets better and better?

Freedom, of course, to identify our own goals—be they personal or professional—and achieve them. Safety and stability. Opportunities to pursue challenges and utilize our skills and talents to their highest and best use. These are the factors that lead to prosperity and happiness in a society.

Our quality of life is directly affected by these factors. But have we seen an upward trend in these areas over the years? No.

Why? It is because society functions only as well as its government functions.

Government is not working anymore.

Governments around the world continue to sink further into debt and dysfunction. Politicians and bureaucrats overpromise and underdeliver. They make decisions that lead to more conflict, more waste, and more pain for us all. Their actions create the kind of instability that makes it hard to find a job. Or keep a job.

There are talented leaders in government. I'm not saying there are no great leaders in government. I am saying that there are too few great leaders in government, and there are forces keeping our greatest leaders out of government.

We have a big problem. In fact, it's our number one problem:

Our #1 problem is that government is on the wrong path,
a path marked by a sign that reads:

> BUREAUCRACY

This path gets muddier and muddier as we go. The burdens and restrictions and waste get worse and worse down this path. If we stay on this path, I fear that one day our shoes will make a sucking sound of finality. We would grunt and strain, but then forward progress would stop. And that dream of life getting better and better? It would come to an end.

You may feel the same way. Three separate polls from Reuters, the *New York Times*, and the *Wall Street Journal* over three months in 2011 found that more than 70 percent of Americans think the country is "on the wrong track."[2] We have been talking about this as a society for decades.

Around the dinner table when I was growing up, my family and I often debated issues related to leadership, government, and freedom. One of the first books my father gave me was *Free to Choose*, which outlines Nobel Prize–winner Milton Friedman's philosophy of how free choice generally leads to better outcomes than the inevitable subpar outcomes produced by a bureaucracy.

Unfortunately, the challenges of fixing government today typically lie in the hands of bureaucratic non-leaders we have put in office. These are people who never had a chance to develop the skill of leadership. People who have not analyzed complex problems, allocated scarce resources to their highest and best uses, and aligned people to take coordinated action to achieve the group's goals. People who are not familiar with best practices of budgeting, hiring, strategic planning, continuous improvement, lean management, process improvement, customer satisfaction, goal-setting, and accountability. These well-intended non-leaders tend to focus on *what's* wrong with government, and on what they need to do to get reelected or reappointed. Their solutions often include short-term answers, increasing restrictions and burdens for one segment of the citizenry or another, new laws designed to overcome the flaws of old laws, and complex regulations. They rely on bureaucracy, and do not have the gift of leadership talent.

Yet we as citizens have a bad habit of turning to these non-leaders again and again to solve our government's most complex leadership problems. It's like we are going to a dentist when we need heart surgery. It is like going to a concert offered by people who have never picked up an instrument prior to opening night. It is like boarding a plane and overhearing one of the pilots say to the other, "Um, hmm, hey Pat, can you tell me again what all of these dials mean, and what these lever thingies do?" Talent matters! So why do we keep putting so many non-leaders into leadership offices?

What keeps us on this bureaucracy path? One core thing. The absence of great leaders in government. And the more dysfunctional government becomes, the more it repels our greatest leaders from wanting to serve in it. It is the Doom Loop of Bureaucracy—the more bureaucratic government becomes, the more it repels the leaders we need to fix it.

But the problem of bureaucratic dysfunction can be solved. I have seen it solved many times—both in the private sector and now in the public sector. It starts by stepping off the path of bureaucracy and choosing a new path. This path is marked by a sign that says:

LEADOCRACY

The Doom Loop of Bureaucracy

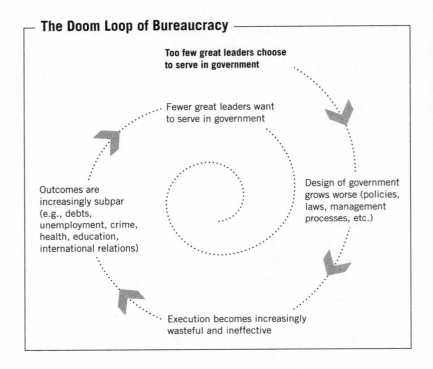

Too few great leaders choose
to serve in government

Fewer great leaders want
to serve in government

Outcomes are
increasingly subpar
(e.g., debts,
unemployment, crime,
health, education,
international relations)

Design of government
grows worse (policies,
laws, management
processes, etc.)

Execution becomes increasingly
wasteful and ineffective

The Solution: Hiring More Great Leaders into Government

I have spent my entire professional life evaluating leaders. It's what I do. And I love this work.

I was born into the hands of an industrial psychologist. Well, the doctor actually did the delivery, but my father cut the cord. My father, Brad Smart, spent *his* career focused on the topic of selecting leaders, so he was my earliest and most profound mentor in this field. Leadership selection was the subject of my Ph.D. dissertation at Claremont, where I had the amazing opportunity of studying under the "Father of Management," Peter Drucker. In my graduate-school apartment in 1995, I founded a leadership consulting firm called ghSMART because I believed that the world would be a better place if organizations did a better job of putting the right *who* in the right *where* doing the right *what* to achieve their goals.

Over nearly two decades, my ghSMART colleagues and I have helped thousands of leaders in all types of organizations across the globe to identify and solve their biggest leadership problems. Problems like "How can I perform at my best as a leader?" Problems like "Who should I hire for this important leadership assignment?" Problems like "How can we transform this three-hundred-year-old struggling company into a high-performing culture that values accountability, innovation, and results?" Harvard University wrote a couple of case studies about our firm, which describe ghSMART as a pioneer in the growing field of leadership consulting. Today, these cases are taught in the classroom to all of Harvard's nine hundred first-year MBAs. This means that I get to show up there once a year and face a grilling of biblical proportions about all of the mistakes I have made as an entrepreneur. But it is fun, and a valuable learning experience hearing your firm's past performance and future strategy debated by some brilliant young minds.

Hiring leaders is the subject of my previous book, *Who: The A Method for Hiring*, which I coauthored with my friend and colleague Randy Street. We are so proud that the ideas in *Who* have made an impact on so many leaders' lives. *Who* became a *New York Times* bestseller in the United States and won several international awards, including being named the number one best business book of the year by Canada's *Globe & Mail* newspaper.

For someone who truly appreciates great leadership when

he sees it, it is painful to watch non-leaders in government messing things up for the rest of us. These are people who are not evil. And I am not mad at them. But many of them have no business being in the positions they occupy.

What I have learned over the years is that great leaders do a better job of analyzing what is needed, carefully allocating scarce resources to their highest and best use with minimal waste, and aligning people to achieve the goals that improve everyone's quality of life. So getting more of them into government might end up being the core solution to society's number one problem: broken government.

In fact, I believe we can sum up that solution with six words:

Hiring more great leaders into government.

You may find this solution obvious. I agree. It is obvious. And it became even more obvious to me the farther I have gone in this journey. This thought crystallized while I was working with Governor Hickenlooper and his dynamic chief of staff, Roxane White. From that point, I spent months testing this solution by chasing down and interviewing some of the great leaders who have actually made the leap into government. I wanted to hear what government was really like. What I discovered was a movement that was already underway. There is already a flow of great leaders from the private sector into the government sector. So I did not start this movement. I am simply giving it a name. And through this book, I am encouraging you to spread the word, so we can amplify this movement—the leadocracy movement.

Leadocracy means "government by society's greatest leaders."

The solution
to our number
one problem:
hiring
more great
leaders into
government.

It is based on the idea that **government is only as good as *who* is in it.**

A society that fields its best leaders into government leadership positions will perform better than a society that does not.

Leadocracy is not a call for a new form of government. Leadocracy is simply the next step in improving the grand experiment known as democracy. Leadocracy is the same form of democracy, or "constitutional republic," that we have in the United States. I like that our citizens freely elect our leaders, and that anybody could become president regardless of race, creed, or family name. Let's keep that. And I like the checks and balances of power, intended to reduce the chance of corruption and tyranny. Let's keep that, too.

The only change that leadocracy suggests to our current model of government is inserting more great leaders into government. Government is not just a collection of laws. *Who* is governing is just as important as the system in which they are governing.

What are the alternative forms of government? Aristocracy? Monarchy (government by birthright)? No, those models are based on entitlement, not talent. Anarchy? Nope, I don't want to live in an anarchy; that is too messy and scary. What about a society governed by "philosopher kings" as Plato suggests in *The Republic*? No, thank you. We do not need more philosophers in government. We need more great leaders.

There are great leaders in our country, people you will hear about throughout the book, who have already made the leap from the private sector into government. And I think when you learn what they are accomplishing, you'll be uplifted and inspired, just as I have been.

Here's the really crazy thing. We have plenty of amazing leaders in society!

I know that great leaders are out there—I've talked to thousands of them! I also know that without the right leadership, most problems go unsolved or get worse. With great leadership, no problem is unsolvable.

Unfortunately, today too few great leaders want to go into government. In a review of the database of CEOs at my firm, ghSMART, a University of Chicago research team led by entrepreneurship professor Steven Kaplan found that only 2 percent of CEOs expressed an interest in going into government during their careers. Only 2 percent! Yikes. The idea of government is so unsavory, it turns off most of our very best leaders. Some of the leaders I talked to actually laughed at me when I asked them if they would ever consider a role in government. As government gets even more dysfunctional, it repels our greatest leaders from ever wanting to serve. But if we can prime the pump and get more great leaders into government, we will be able to reverse the Doom Loop of Bureaucracy. We can begin gaining momentum with the Virtuous Cycle of Leadocracy.

Mostly, leadocracy is a call to action. To select government leaders more intelligently. To encourage the great leaders you know to apply their talents in the public sector at some point during their careers. To urge society's greatest leaders to consider taking a leadership adventure by doing a stint in public service at some point in their careers.

The purpose of this book is to help get us out of the dysfunctional Doom Loop of Bureaucracy and to amplify the Virtuous Cycle of Leadocracy that is already underway.

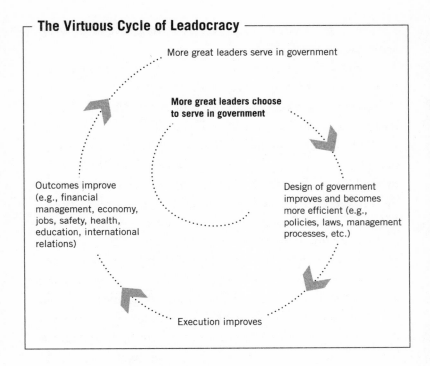

The Virtuous Cycle of Leadocracy

More great leaders serve in government

More great leaders choose to serve in government

Outcomes improve (e.g., financial management, economy, jobs, safety, health, education, international relations)

Design of government improves and becomes more efficient (e.g., policies, laws, management processes, etc.)

Execution improves

Outline

What I found when I first got to go "behind the scenes" in government shocked me. I'll tell you about that experience in chapter 1.

Fearing that my experience as leadership advisor to Governor Hickenlooper and Chief of Staff Roxane White was an anomaly, I asked them to connect me with other private sector leaders who had made the leap into government. They did. So I got to talk candidly with top government leaders in other geographies—leaders like Governors Mitch Daniels of Indiana and Jack Markell of Delaware. Heck, I even called up the top positive psychology researcher in the world, Mihaly Csikszentmihalyi, to ask him whether he thought that private sector leaders might experience more career satisfaction doing a stint in government, or whether this assumption was foolish to even suggest. What he told me actually gave me the chills.

In talking with all of these interesting, "in the know" people, the goal was to answer three burning questions:

1. Is government too broken, or can great leaders actually make a difference?
2. What are the obstacles preventing more great leaders from going into government, and how might we remove them?
3. For the leaders who make the leap into government, do they regret it? Or did they find the experience worth it?

Around the time I was unexpectedly thrust into this world of government, I had already begun working on a new book project on business leadership, called *The Ideal Leader*, with my ghSMART colleagues Randy Street and Alan Foster. We are redefining what great leadership in the private sector means. We call the essence of leadership the "3 As of Leadership"— analyzing, allocating, and aligning. Rather than make you wait a few years for that book's release, I'll give you a preview of this framework as it applies to leadership in government in chapter 2.

Of course, the first hurdle I considered when I thought about getting more great leaders into government was the question of where they would come from. In chapter 3, I'll talk about the fact that we have a vast resource of talented, experienced leaders in the private sector of our country, and that we've already seen private sector leaders do great things in government leadership positions.

Identifying great leaders is one thing. Getting them to serve is something entirely different. When I talked to leaders whom I thought could make improvements in government, most of them said they wouldn't do it. In chapter 4, I'll share the most common obstacles they said made them avoid government. I'll then reveal stories from leaders in government that will help you sort myth from reality. In chapter 5, we'll hear what the benefits are to the individual leader of serving in government. I'll show that it's linked to this concept of "flow," the essence of happiness at work according to renowned psychologist Mihaly Csikszentmihalyi.

In chapter 6, I'll offer some simple tools you can use to spot great leaders and elect them. I'll introduce the Leadocracy Scorecard, which is like a checklist that you can use to evaluate candidates to decide who deserves your vote.

In chapter 7, I'll tell you about what I'm doing to try to advance the leadocracy movement. It's not the only solution. In fact, if this became the only organization supporting leadocracy, I would be disappointed. But it's my "putting my money where my mouth is"—100 percent of my author royalties from this book are being donated to this not-for-profit organization. It is called The Leaders Initiative. It is a not-for-profit organization whose mission is "to elevate humanity by identifying, developing, and deploying society's greatest leaders into government." That sounds lofty, and it is, but we are off to a good start. It's just one way to get the Virtuous Cycle of Leadocracy spinning faster and harder for all of our benefit. The Leaders Initiative is kind of like Teach for America, but rather than putting twenty-one-year-olds into low-income schools for two-year teaching stints, we put highly accomplished private sector leaders into two-year government leadership stints. I've already signed the Leadocracy Pledge—to do a two-year full-time leadership job myself in government by my seventieth birthday (see page 143). I hope you will, too, and to encourage the best private sector leaders you know to do so.

Finally, in chapter 8, I'll share more stories of the real-world achievements that great private sector leaders have made in government, to attempt to persuade you that leadocracy isn't a pipe dream. These individuals are already creating communities that are safer, that are more financially stable and designed for economic growth, and that provide greater quality of life for citizens.

The leadocracy movement is underway. I hope that when you finish this book, you'll tell everybody you know to read it and contribute to the most important movement of our generation.

• • •

I believe that leadership is the ultimate lever for good in the world.

I believe that great leaders elevate humanity. I've met people who believe the same and are acting on those beliefs. People who are steering their communities onto the path of leadocracy.

The leadocracy movement has the potential to become like the Space Race of the second half of the last century. Consider the parallels. Each is a difficult but not impossible challenge that is worth doing. We flew a person to the moon and back in the 1960s! That was an incredible feat.

But this time, rather than competing for supremacy in space, perhaps nations will consider competing for the greatest number of talented leaders serving in government. And a rising tide of leadership competence in government will raise all boats. The leadocracy movement is more important than the Space Race. It's more important than reducing the national debt. It's more important than global trade, the environment, and world health.

Leadocracy is *how* all of these problems will be solved most effectively. Bureaucracy will not get us there. Leadocracy will.

How do we make it happen? That is what this book is all about. It is a great pleasure and privilege to share my discoveries along this journey with you.

Once we start hiring more great leaders into government, life will just get better and better. Yours. Mine. All of ours.

CHAPTER 1

Who, Not What

*Laws and institutions must go hand in hand with the progress
of the human mind. As that becomes more developed,
more enlightened . . . institutions must advance also,
and keep pace with the times.*
—*Thomas Jefferson*[3]

On a cold day in December of 2010, I received the following
email from a client:

> *Geoff,*
>
> *As you might be aware, I am on the governor-elect's transi-
> tion team. Various lawyers and professionals are donating
> hundreds of hours. Would your firm be prepared to inter-
> view two to three of the top candidates for various cabinet
> positions? We would need this done in the next couple of
> weeks, as they are making the announcements by year-end.
> Roxane White, chief of staff, would like to call you.*
>
> *Thanks in advance. The People of Colorado appreciate your
> support.*
>
> *Blair Richardson*

My initial reaction was, "No way!"

Various thoughts crossed my mind. *Help the government? Government is hopeless and broken. What's the point? We're on a path to inevitable doom. Eventually, if it gets bad enough, I'll have to move my family to Australia or somewhere.*

Any help I offer to the new governor would be pointless. All of his leadership hiring decisions will be politically motivated anyway.

The next couple of weeks? It's December 13! I was planning on coasting into the New Year and eating myself into a pleasant holiday stupor, maybe doing some shopping with the family. Bad timing. Too bad, so sad.

I'm going to say no.

That's what I thought. I started writing back with my regrets. "I'm sorry, but—"

My fingers froze on the keyboard.

A thought had popped into my head. Blair is somebody for whom I have the utmost respect. He radiates success— kind, polite, and never too busy to forget to put a tri-fold pocket square in his blazer. He's smart, has delivered impressive results as a global business leader, has a great family, and so on. *If* he *is helping, maybe the situation isn't hopeless,* I thought. Besides, *Time* magazine had called the new governor, John Hickenlooper, one of the "Five Best Big-City Mayors" in his previous job as mayor of Denver, and he had been a business leader and entrepreneur before that. I realized that I wouldn't mind meeting him. In fact, it was a rare opportunity to meet a fellow businessperson who had gone into public service. I was curious what it was like. And I was interested in meeting our new governor, to see what he was all about. I had voted for him, after all.

I deleted the words I had written, and wrote this instead:

Yes.

I voted for Hickenlooper, and am happy to use my firm's expertise to help him pick a great cabinet. His success as our governor will be largely determined by the quality of the team he selects. Privileged to serve.

The work I was about to do for the governor ended up being the most exciting, meaningful, and fun work I did all year. And I can point to it as the moment that put me on the path to a very different mind-set about government and how to improve it.

A Journey Begins

Four days after I sent the reply, I found myself at a small round conference table with John Hickenlooper, the newly elected governor of my home state of Colorado, and his chief of staff, Roxane White. Our task was to discuss whom to hire for key cabinet roles. The governor was to take office in three weeks.

In person, Governor Hickenlooper looked like the brew pub owner that he once was—energetic, friendly, and genuine. A mop of semi-combed hair flopped around cheerfully as he spoke. But I noticed an intensity of purpose behind his eyes, which let me know that we had important business to attend to today. And Roxane White—I was not sure what to expect from this former not-for-profit CEO and social-services director. Was she going to be a bleeding heart? I had heard that she was tough as nails. Was she going to be that in a good way, or a pain to work with? What I found was a woman who matched the governor on energy, but managed to steer hers, and his, into lanes of highly productive decision making.

Instantly, I could see why they made a great pair in their previous jobs as mayor of Denver and mayoral chief of staff.

Would this be a formal and stilted conversation? I had wondered how this governor would respond to my business-oriented approach to leadership selection. I was expecting this to be a waste of his time and mine. Any moment, I would hear the words or see the actions that would confirm my assumption that all government was dysfunctional beyond any hope of repair. But I was in for a surprise.

While the mood was serious, it was also refreshingly upbeat and practical. Governor Hickenlooper was engaged and clearly determined to make the best possible leadership decisions for key roles in his cabinet. The discussion about candidates was focused, fact-based, and lively. We focused on one key role at a time. What was the mission for the role? Key outcomes to achieve? Competencies that matter in that role? What about the slate of candidates? What are their backgrounds? To what extent do we have data to suggest how strong or weak they are on our scorecard checklist areas? What remaining questions need to be addressed before the in-depth interview?

The chief of staff had a refreshing can-do attitude in the face of this daunting challenge. Once we covered a topic thoroughly, we shifted seamlessly to the next topic of importance. *These people are as sharp as any of my CEO or private-equity clients. This is going really well. Oh my gosh*, I admitted to myself, *I am actually having fun.*

The governor's leadership competence began to chip away at my negative assumptions. First, he was clearly more interested in hiring the best leader than in playing politics. He didn't make any references to political party during these discussions.

Not once. Let me repeat that: We spent hours discussing key hires for cabinet roles. Not one time did the governor say the word *Republican* or *Democrat*. That was mind-blowing to me; I assumed that every elected leader cared mostly about the politics surrounding appointment decisions.

Second, he had his eye on results. What were we trying to achieve in human services, by when? How much would that cost? It was a very straightforward discussion of outcomes and strategies, not too different from thousands of conversations I have had with leaders in the private sector. Then he really surprised me and started talking about customers.

When I heard the governor refer to citizens as "customers," I almost fell out of my swivel chair. Our citizens are our customers. We are here because they put us here. How do we take their tax revenue and invest it as wisely as possible? How do we manage those investments of time and money as intelligently as possible to deliver the best results?

I was shocked. And the second thing that I felt was a sense of relief. *Maybe the situation in government is not hopeless*, I thought.

All was going well, but then something happened.

Flipping through some of the résumés for one cabinet position, I began to feel disheartened. The job we were discussing was a big one. It required managing a multibillion-dollar business unit, or department, in the government. Thousands of employees. Weak performance outcomes. It was a big leadership responsibility to turn this organization around. "There are a few impressive candidates in the stack, but too few," I said. "Where's the A list?" I asked with my palms open, hoping not to insult anybody. I then added, with a smile on my face to bring some levity to my question, "Do you have some secret drawer somewhere where you keep all the great résumés? You know, people who have actually managed a $3 billion P&L before, and have led thousands of employees successfully?"

The governor and his chief of staff cried out, almost in unison, "We can't get enough of the kind of leaders you are talking about. They won't come!"

The governor continued, "I would love nothing better than to hire the very best leaders we have in our state. But they have a perception that government is unsavory, so they won't come."

Before I could stop myself, I blurted out, "*Isn't* government unsavory?" My face got red as I realized how insulting it sounded.

The governor was not fazed by my question. "It doesn't have to be," Governor Hickenlooper replied with a small smile.

"In our administration, we're going to be all about talent and results. We are going to make government the 3 Es— more elegant, effective, and efficient. So it will be a lot less unsavory for my key leaders here than in an administration that was all about politics. In the right situation, a cabinet job like this can actually be incredibly rewarding and meaningful for a leader."

So all government roles are not unsavory. OK. Hmm. Maybe more leaders would go into government if we let them know that this is true. But right now, we clearly have an absence of great leaders.

That's why government is so messed up, I thought.

I asked, "So what if you *could* get all the great leaders you want? Let's say I backed a school bus up to your door right there, and it was filled with the state's greatest leaders, eager to accept positions in your administration?"

The governor quickly replied, "Well, you would have a

government that performed much, much better. There is no question about that. The change would be profound."

That is when it really clicked. Yes, government is broken; everyone knows that. Our attempts to fix it have been focused on chasing *what* solutions—new laws, regulations, fiddling with policies, arguing about ideology. But what if the fundamental problem were not a what problem? What if the fundamental problem were a *who* problem?

What if the fundamental problem was simply that we did not have enough great leaders in government? *Then it would make sense for us to stop chasing the what, and solve the who,* I thought. That point is in the last sentence of *Who*, the book I coauthored. It was echoing in my head as I sat there.

Stop chasing the what. Solve the who.

I looked at the governor and his chief of staff and, choosing my words carefully as I counted out six fingers, I said, "Hiring. More. Great. Leaders. Into. Government. There is a six-word solution to the problem of how to reform government. I shrugged my shoulders to invite honest feedback. "Right?"

Five seconds of silence.

Then the governor replied, "Yes."

That December day, in that room with the governor, something told me that this solution did not apply just to our state but also could apply to all governments everywhere. Getting more great leaders into government could improve the quality of life of people around the world. OK, that might be a fundamental solution. But how to make that happen? "Someone should develop a program to get those leaders in office," I said. "You could just go get them. You could demystify government for them. You could train them. Then they do a stint. You could begin at the state level. And if it worked, the idea could spread to other states, and then to the federal and local levels, and then to other countries."

"Like Teach for America," Chief of Staff White added.

"They could do a stint for a couple of years," said the governor, "and if they want to stay in it, they could; or they could then roll off back into the private sector. It's not like they would have to spend the rest of their career in government."

Silence. Exchange of looks. We were playing a game of "who's going to step up?" The governor's expression—eyes wide open, eyebrows arched—told me what he was thinking: *OK, Mr. Bright Idea Guy, I'm serving as governor. I'm already doing my part. What are you going to do to help the cause?*

I knew he would need someone to get such a program up and running. Someone who was a believer in the power of great leadership. Someone who could help to bridge great leaders from the private sector into the public sector. *Oh my gosh, that would take a lot of time if you do it right*, I thought. *I can't believe what I'm about to offer. Here, I have been skeptical about government for forty years. And now, after one enjoyable meeting with an enlightened governor, I'm going to offer to start some government reform initiative?*

I didn't even wait for him to vocalize the need.

"I'll do it," I said. (Gulp.) And "it" turned into two things: (1) the book you hold in your hands, and (2) The Leaders Initiative, which is described in chapter 7.

Why Leaders Are the Solution

I'm passionate about great leaders. I have seen many times how great leaders can turn around or improve organizations. And when you have the wrong leader or leaders, no amount of policy change or strategizing makes a darn bit of difference. Governor Hickenlooper seemed like he really "got it." So did his chief of staff.

However, while I was walking back to my car after that meeting, I felt a wave of doubt sweep over me. You know that feeling when you've just committed to do something big and scary, and you're starting to wonder if it was such a great idea after all? *Just because I have a passion for leadership doesn't mean that it's the solution to society's problems*, I thought. You've heard the saying by the psychologist Abraham Maslow, "If the only tool you have is a hammer, everything looks like a nail." *Maybe I'm a leadership junkie, so the only solution to fixing government I see is leadership. And maybe all of the leadership success stories I've witnessed in the business world aren't relevant to the world of government. Maybe it's not a good solution. Maybe I'm not the guy.*

In Jim Collins's landmark book *Good to Great* (2001), he urges leaders to focus on "First Who . . . Then What." My book *Who* outlines a step-by-step approach to achieving the goal of successful hiring with 90 percent accuracy. But I wondered whether this fundamental solution for business applied to government.

And yet, a friend had once come to me with a very similar idea. Mark Gallogly serves on President Obama's Council on Jobs and Competitiveness and was a senior managing director with the investment firm Blackstone Group before he cofounded Centerbridge Partners. Years ago, he recommended that I read Ben Franklin's autobiography and emulate Franklin's practice of getting talented people from commerce together to discuss issues of the day from a civic perspective and engage in problem solving. Mark is incredibly smart. As I recalled his counsel, I felt encouraged that I was on the right track.

And when I considered what I'd seen leaders accomplish when the *who* got solved before trying to tackle the *what*, I felt even more confident.

I have witnessed many versions of the following story. The members of the board of directors of a company are sitting around a large, shiny, wooden boardroom table. The conversation is going down the wrong path. They are taking a *what* approach to trying to diagnose and to fix a troubled company. The company has been struggling for several years. The CEO is asked to step out for the last half-hour so the board could talk candidly about the dire situation. The discussion among board members goes something like this: One board member says, "We clearly have a *financial* problem—margins are falling and our revenue is not meeting forecast either. I have some ideas about what we can do financially to right the ship." Another says, "No, we have a *product* problem—we are getting beaten on quality and we aren't positioning our core products right. We need to execute a whole product overhaul." And another says, "It's actually a *sales* problem—we just don't have the right sales process in place." I raise my hand and say, "You are wisely pointing out many *what* problems that this company is facing. But the job of the board is to make one great *who* decision—to hire the right CEO. Based on our analysis, you have a CEO problem. My recommendation is to focus your energy on hiring the right CEO, and then let that person fix all of these other problems you have identified." The board eventually takes advice. And it works. The new CEO hires more great people. He or she articulates clear goals to the organization, puts in place a plan to improve products and processes, executes with urgency and accountability, and the financial performance improves. I have seen this pattern many times. If you fix the *who* problem, the what problems get better. What would stop great leaders from improving government in the same way?

I had to find out whether the principle applied in government. Because I was a newbie to government, I needed input from people with more experience. What if I could identify and interview great leaders in government to find out what their context was really like?

I was able to track down and talk to some amazing leaders. These conversations took me on an incredible journey of discovery. I'll share that journey throughout the book, but my discussions with these great leaders ultimately boiled down to three big insights: Great leaders tackle challenges head on. Great leaders are talent magnets. And great leaders deliver great results for stakeholders, sometimes against long odds. Given our current problems and level of dysfunction, we need great leaders in government now more than ever.

Great Leaders Tackle Challenges

"One of the things that I have always been attracted to are long odds." That sentence from my talk with Governor Jack Markell of Delaware energized me. It was the opposite of what I expect to hear from a politician. Or at least it is the opposite of the behavior I expect from them. I think most people feel that politicians talk a big game, but when it comes time to really tackle a challenge, they shy away out of fear of alienating voters.

Clearly, Governor Markell was different. His voice even sounded different from most politicians. He made clear points. He backed up his points with data. He sounded comfortable in his own skin—no need to overexplain, no excessive need to be liked, no used-car-salesman slickery.

"People in government are inclined not to take risks, because if they make a mistake it could be used against them in a campaign or they could read about it on the front page of the paper. And so one of my most important responsibilities as governor is to encourage the state employees and others to take healthy risks. You always try to minimize and mitigate the risk, but you've got to tackle challenges. If you don't you're not going to get ahead."

That approach has lead Jack Markell to continued success as governor. In his first year alone, he successfully tackled three intense challenges: he balanced the state budget despite an $800 million deficit without laying off employees, he boosted educational initiatives, and he increased environmental protections. This is an amazing performance, especially compared to what most governors achieve in their first year in office.

Bold moves in the right direction were a consistent theme in my conversations with the amazing leaders I talked to. The state of Michigan has faced many challenges as the auto industry has evolved, leaving unemployment high and the state's finances in shambles for many years. Imagine being elected governor of Michigan. I could not imagine it. So I asked him myself what it was like. And I was surprised by his upbeat and positive attitude.

Governor Rick Snyder of Michigan had taken office less than a year before I talked with him. His voice squeaked a bit with excitement when he got to the punch line of his stories. The thing that struck me first was the positive attitude he maintained, despite being at the helm of one of the most challenged states in the union.

Governor Snyder told me that he has a phrase that drives him: "relentless positive action," or RPA. He chose a solution-oriented approach. And he knew that he needed top talent to make a dent in improving his state's grim situation— a massive budget deficit, ten years of recession, a low ranking in terms of most economic indicators. "I looked at the candidate pool," he told me, "and there were some good, well-intentioned people. But they were career politicians, and my view was that they would try to fix things through incrementalism. My mantra, my vision, was to *reinvent Michigan*. So I believed we needed leaders from the outside to challenge the norm and say, 'The traditional ways of doing things are not good enough.' I was hired, and that's the way I describe it, for this job to follow through on what I ran on, and it's about solving problems."

And Governor Snyder has solved problems. In just eleven months, he balanced the budget and instituted a number of other amazing improvements that I will describe throughout the book. Get this: under Governor Snyder's leadership, Bloomberg News recently placed Michigan in the number two spot in their ranking of the fifty states by economic health. He has more challenges to face, but he is off to a great start.

As a leader of a massively complex organization, you can never be sure of the final results of your decisions. But if you avoid the important and difficult challenges, the organization will never be able to reverse the Doom Loop of Bureaucracy.

Great Leaders Are Talent Magnets

Mitch Daniels has built an astounding record of success as governor of Indiana. I had heard of him for years. My friends in Chicago have such profound respect for his reputation that they joke that they would love to outsource the management of the state of Illinois to the state of Indiana under Governor

Daniels. But people who don't know of his great track record tend to undervalue his leadership. A New York friend of mine told me once, "I saw that guy Mitch Daniels speak. Not exciting enough. His speech wasn't very entertaining. He'll never be elected president." I asked, "Do you have any idea what he has achieved in Indiana? And besides, would you rather have a government that is entertaining, or a government that delivers great results?" My friend did not choose to respond.

Governor Daniels has defied everything I previously assumed about government and the futility of trying to improve it.

He balanced the budget, upgraded services, put a greater focus on public safety and on children's welfare. The list goes on. Under his leadership, multiple agencies developed award-winning approaches that other states began to emulate. I knew he was somebody I had to talk to.

Thanks to an introduction by my governor, Governor Daniels agreed to a call with me. It was a call I knew I wouldn't be able to reschedule. Not with all of the priorities on his calendar. So you can imagine how stressed I was when my wife broke her nose in a weight-lifting accident and was scheduled to have surgery during the exact time of my call with Governor Daniels. Instead of rescheduling the call, I recruited my wife's brother to be my "stunt double" and stand by her bedside for forty-five minutes during her recovery while I snuck out into the parking lot and dialed in. The call proved to be nothing short of inspirational, and further disproved my assumption that government was hopeless and doomed to an eternity of dysfunction.

"I can remember so many nights giving some speech, getting all wound up," Governor Daniels said of his time on the campaign trail. "I'd say, 'I just know that if people of change can break through, individuals of outstanding talent and idealism will step forward to help us.' And then I'd walk out to the RV and think, 'Big mouth, how do you know that?' But it happened. It really did happen." One of those individuals of outstanding talent is Earl Goode, whom you will meet later in this book. The governor described in detail how he put together what sounds to me like an all-star team of leaders. "We ended up putting together an outstanding group of people," Governor Daniels said. "It made all the difference."

Great leaders are talent magnets. They're focused on talent because they recognize that the best way to improve performance is to build teams with the most talented people. They recognize talent when it's in front of them and scoop it up. They hunt talent down and do what's necessary to bring great contributors on board. Governor Jack Markell of Delaware told me he brought in people from every age group and from every sector as he built his administration, to get a range of experience and an infusion of new ideas.

Talented people want to work with great leaders. They know that their skills will be put to good use, that they will be challenged, that they'll be given new opportunities.

I'll tell you more about what Governor Daniels has achieved in later chapters. But one thing was clear—he credited the talent in his administration for those successes. "A huge advantage for us was that in our administration, essentially everybody was new. I'm not sure we had anybody who had been in government before. And that was a big plus because they came in with what the Chinese call 'young eyes.' They asked all the right questions: 'Why do we do that? Why don't we try something else?'"

So when you put a Mitch Daniels into office, you don't get just one great leader. That one great leader will attract dozens or even hundreds of other highly talented people. And highly talented leaders produce something more than the hot air, scandals, and dysfunction that bureaucrats tend to produce. They produce results.

Great Leaders Deliver Great Results

Fred Steingraber wanted to accomplish something simple. He wanted to figure out what the citizens of Kenilworth, Illinois, wanted. Then he wanted to find a way to deliver it. Fred has a round and wise face, and wears rectangular glasses. His voice has a little bit of drama in it, and he sounds a bit like the old sports announcer Howard Cosell.

"First of all, we are going to develop a set of priorities," he told the village board soon after being elected as president (which is like the role of mayor). "Some of these priorities will involve significant time investment, and perhaps money. We want to understand what should be getting the most attention from the village staff and what the residents expect from us in terms of quality, service, and costs. I want a high level of transparency with regard to how we are allocating our resources. Second, we will not raise taxes before we have explored every option for reducing our costs. And third, transparency is absolutely critical in everything we do."

Transparency is terrifying to many in leadership positions. Why? Because it only highlights how poor their results are! But for great leaders, transparency is a must. Great leaders are focused on delivering outstanding results. And transparency helps citizens or customers understand how well their needs are being met. "We communicate regularly on what's happening, what work is being done, what results we're getting, the costs, what the time table is for completing projects, and so on," Fred told me.

I could tell you many stories of amazing results that are actually being delivered by government leaders right now. Balanced budgets. Better services. Less waste. Higher standards of living. Unfortunately, they're not being delivered everywhere. Not in most places. The Founding Fathers—Jefferson, Washington, Franklin, etc.—were a talented bunch of leaders. I believe that the Founding Fathers wanted checks and balances, so that power would never be too concentrated in the hands of tyrants. That makes sense. But there is no way that they wanted the accumulation of waste and inefficiency and dysfunction that now plagues our government. And it is no coincidence that we are not fielding a team in government these days that is anywhere as talented as the team that started this grand experiment of democracy back in 1776.

I asked Joe Scarlett, the legendary retired chairman of the Tractor Supply Company and founder of the Scarlett Leadership Institute, what he thought about the quality of leaders in government today. Joe has a big, booming, grandfatherly voice. He repeated the question I had just asked him. "Do I think we have our best leaders in government? No, I don't think so at all. I don't think we're coming close.

"In any organization, whether it's government or business or nonprofit, the better the quality of leadership, the more effective the organization's going to be—no matter what," Joe said. "The quality of the leadership reflects on the performance of the organization. A good leader sets the direction and the value structure, and then empowers his people. In government today, there's really no clear leadership, there's no clear direction, and there's no value structure."

The absence of great leaders in government is why we are in the situation we are in. Therefore, let's change our focus from chasing the *what*—regulations, laws, policies, ideology—and solve the *who*.

The Leadocracy Discussion

1. Fixing government is a "chicken or the egg" problem. Do you start with the *who*, or do you start with the *what*? What do you think?

2. What matters more to you, leadership talent or political ideology? In other words, who would you rather have representing you—someone who fits your political ideology exactly, but who has only modest leadership talent? Or someone who does not fit your political ideology exactly, but who has demonstrated exceptional leadership talent in their career?

3. In what ways do you think government is like the private sector and therefore should operate as such, and in what ways do you think government requires a different playbook for success?

CHAPTER 2

The 3 As of Leadership

If your actions inspire others to dream more, learn more,
do more, and become more, you are a leader.
—*John Quincy Adams*

"It's probably the most important thing we've done that will never be talked about." Earl Goode (rhymes with "food") is Governor Mitch Daniels's chief of staff. When he said this to me, I had no idea what story he was going to tell, but I knew that it was going to be good. As it turns out, his story illustrates how leadership is really a set of behaviors that lead to results.

Leadership is not a state of "being"; it is a state of "doing." Earl told his story with his down-home accent. His voice was smooth and clear, and he did not attempt to hide emotion when he felt it might give weight to his point.

Earl began working with Governor Daniels as head of the Department of Administration, responsible for procurement, personnel, IT, and a host of other items. What he found was a highly inefficient, uncoordinated, wasteful bureaucracy. "When Mitch became governor," said Earl, "we had seventy or eighty independent, autonomous agencies. We had dozens of different email systems, dozens of different voicemail systems.

We did not have an accounting system that was common to all executive branch agencies. We didn't have a common personnel system. Most agencies had their own chief information officer, personnel director, their own legal counsel, and so forth. The only thing that might be common to all agencies was some statute passed by the legislature.

"Each agency made its own procurement decisions, and within some of the larger agencies, we had multiple locations around the state making independent procurement decisions, for fuel, commodities, and everything else.

"Now we operate as one enterprise," Earl explained. "We have one financial system. We have one personnel system. We centralized IT. So we have real-time financials and real-time mechanized procurement. And we're doing more with less in almost every agency."

The results have been remarkable in making government perform better for less money. Governor Daniels's administration saved well over $30 million annually just through centralized, strategic sourcing. They initiated a "Buy Indiana" program and raised the percent of dollars spent with in-state companies from 60 to 90 percent. From 2004 to 2010, payroll and benefits dropped by more than $100 million. The move to centralize administrative responsibilities helped take the state from a massive deficit to a surplus of about $1.2 billion in just two years, without tax increases.

Real-time performance monitoring is one feature of the Mitch Daniels approach to management. But this approach is not shared in most other states. "One of our cabinet members was recruited to a much larger state than ours," said Earl. "He was back for a visit a couple of months later, and I asked him how it was going. 'One thing is really different,' he said.

'When I did something in my agency you guys knew about it within twenty-four hours. Now, it might be three years before they know what I've done.'"

Earl laughed when he told this part of the story, but I had a hard time laughing with him. I thought, *How many communities is this happening in, where the left hand doesn't know what the right hand is doing? Or worse, where the head doesn't know what any of the hands is doing?*

The more I talked to leaders inside government, the more I recognized ideas that I was currently exploring with my colleagues at ghSMART. I realized that our framework for leadership applies just as well in the government context as it does in business and not-for-profit contexts. Or any other context in which humans are leading other humans, for that matter.

We don't think of leadership as some set of fuzzy, intangible character qualities that some people are born with and others are not. We think of leadership as the performance of behaviors. The skill of performing these behaviors can be learned and developed by anybody. Some people do not develop these skills and therefore do not perform leader behaviors with much competence. Others develop some skill and become pretty good leaders. Others develop considerable skill and become great leaders.

Let's define *great leader* so it is clear what we are talking about.

A great leader helps a group of people identify what they want and how to get it, and then influences that group, free of coercion, to take coordinated action to achieve the desired outcomes. A great leader achieves results at a level far beyond what others achieve.

Serving as a leader is one of the most challenging and

The 3 As of Leadership:

Analyzing—Figuring out what outcomes are desired and how to achieve them.

Allocating—Establishing a plan to concentrate scarce resources, like money, time, and people, toward their highest and best uses, and away from areas of waste.

Aligning—Influencing people to behave in a coordinated way, according to the plan, to achieve the desired outcomes.

generous things a person can do for another person or group of people. Leaders elevate the human condition. They make things work better. They improve situations that seem dire or hopeless.

They save lives.

Consider some of the world's recent great leaders. Nelson Mandela. Steve Jobs. Mother Theresa. Bill Gates. They all used their leadership talents—diverse as they may be—to make lives better in some way: achieving freedom, making advanced technology available to all of us, improving living conditions in low-income communities, creating a global foundation that propels the idea that all lives have equal value.

But what do great leaders *do* to achieve great results?

The 3 As of Leadership

You've probably heard of the "Three Rs" of education—reading, 'riting, and 'rithmetic. They are the foundational building blocks for the education system globally.

Likewise, leadership has three building blocks. At ghSMART, we call these three modes of behavior the "3 As of Leadership."

The 3 As of Leadership

Analyzing—Figuring out what outcomes are desired and how to achieve them.

Allocating—Establishing a plan to concentrate scarce resources, like money, time, and people, toward their highest and best uses, and away from areas of waste.

Aligning—Influencing people to behave in a coordinated way, according to the plan, to achieve the desired outcomes.

My ghSMART colleagues and I have discovered that a great leader must do these three things very well to achieve the best results possible.

Earl Goode's and Mitch Daniels's transformation of Indiana's disparate agencies into one enterprise is an example of the 3 As of Leadership. Extensive *analyzing* was required to understand the nature of the problem, to understand what tasks might be centralized and what tasks couldn't be. Their next step was *allocating* resources across agencies to eliminate redundancies and improve efficiencies. To execute their new plan required *aligning* all of the agencies and their employees, people whose day-to-day work would deliver the desired results.

Now, more than ever, we need leaders who are highly skilled at the 3 As in the public sector, for the good of us all. These 3 As at the disposal of a great leader are like the ivories in the hands of a concert pianist who is performing your favorite piece of music. They are like the tools in the hand of a master carpenter who is building a cabinet in your kitchen. They are like the medical instruments in the hands of a top surgeon who is repairing a hole in your loved one's heart.

Identifying the 3 As took us sixteen years, thousands of in-depth assessments of leaders, research by Steven Kaplan at the University of Chicago, and original interviews with dozens of entrepreneurs, CEOs, and leaders from all sectors, including education, the government, the military, and the not-for-profit world. In the end, we distilled all of the complexity of leadership down to these three modes of behavior. Our book on this topic, tentatively titled *The Ideal Leader*, is forthcoming.

The leadocracy movement is so important, though, I did not want to make you wait to get the gist of the 3 As. Here is a bit of insight into what the 3 As look like, what they feel like, and how to use them to spot or serve as a great leader in government.

Analyzing

Before Fred Steingraber became president of the village of Kenilworth, Illinois, he led a Blue Ribbon Commission strategy study for the town to stem three consecutive years of deficits. The purpose of this study was to develop a plan to achieve sustainable balanced budgets in the years to come. As he launched the commission, he was met by some political resistance to his fact-based, problem-solving approach.

Without making any personal attacks, Fred said to his fellow commission members, "Look, we have to have an understanding about how we are going to conduct this study. Irrespective of what opinions or biases any of us might have, the only way we can advance the ball down the field is if we do it on the basis of facts and data. On good research. We're going to have to do survey work to understand the merits of different approaches." His colleagues eventually warmed to the idea of doing a needs analysis and quality survey.

"We did a comprehensive survey of all residents in the village asking them to rank and rate the quality of all of the services provided," Fred told me. "I was trying to identify the big gaps—the things that are rated most important, but that are also rated low in terms of quality or service."

Simultaneously, Fred led the commission to gather benchmark data from other communities. They could use this information to evaluate their own costs, services provided, productivity, and the like. It took almost seventeen months, but in the end, the commission was able to make clear recommendations for identifying priorities, improving services, and balancing the budget.

Great leaders start by analyzing the needs and priorities of their constituent group. They analyze the factors inside of the group that might affect the outcome of any decision or strategy. And, they benchmark their relative standing compared to peers. Finally, and most importantly in the village of Kenilworth, they shared this information with their residents.

Analyzing "feels" like studying something to understand it. It is a messy and exploratory process. It might seem like detective work. The leader generates insights through talking with people on the ground, through research, through reviewing numbers and information, through contemplating the nature of a problem or an opportunity. And then she tests hypotheses about what is real.

At the end of the day, analyzing helps the leader find answers to the right questions. Questions like "Why isn't our product selling?" or "Why are so many of our children dropping out of school?" or "How do we balance the budget and keep citizens happy?"

Leaders who don't spend enough time analyzing are said to leap before they look. And those who spend too much are said to suffer from analysis paralysis. Weak analyzing often leads to solving minor problems first (because it's easier to find a solution) rather than identifying the problems at the heart of the success or failure of the community.

Great analyzers ask a lot of questions and listen carefully to the answers, at least according to Governor Jack Markell of Delaware. "I think one of the most important leadership skills that I have is being a good listener. It starts with knowing what questions to ask, and I ask a lot of questions. I'm always trying to dig to the next layer, to really understand what people are trying to achieve and how we can get there. I tolerate a lot of pushback when I'm figuring out what the right solution is, what other questions we should be asking, why I might be looking at this the wrong way. I'm not at all looking for 'yes' people."

The power of listening came through in Earl Goode's early impressions of Governor Mitch Daniels, too. "What really struck me was not what he said, but the way he listened. I mean, you could watch as he processed questions, and his answers were thoughtful, not just rhetoric. I thought to myself then, if I ever were to do something in government, I could work for that guy."

Leaders who are especially good at analyzing are often spoken of as "visionaries" or "strategists." These types of leaders tend to have very high IQs. And they may come off as kind of nerdy. In government, that is a problem. As voters, we often don't value this analyzing skill set as much as we value the ability to give a good speech. Therefore, we don't elect talented analyzers as often as we should.

When our society needs to figure out its priorities and identify the right solutions to complex problems, we need some big-brained analyzers on the job.

Think Bill Gates.

I once saw Bill Gates give a talk at a TED conference. He asked the audience to think about all of the analyzing going on in and around Microsoft. Microsoft has many, many, many IQ points focused on analyzing its internal and external environments, coming up with solutions to maximize the company's performance—company executives, industry analysts, the financial community, its board of directors, customer groups, etc. Gates went on to say that most people he knew assumed that there was a correspondingly robust "brain trust" in government (he was referring specifically to state governments). He took a couple of steps across the stage in silence. "But there is no brain trust," he concluded, and the crowd laughed in nervous agreement.

"But there is no brain trust."

Bill Gates's point reminded me of *Indiana Jones and the Temple of Doom*. Remember the part where the bad guys had already bailed out of the plane, leaving the plane pilot-less and on a collision course with the mountain? A woman in an evening gown realizes this, looks in horror at the empty flight deck, and starts shaking Indiana awake and yelling in his face, "No one's flying the plane!"

Yet, even given Bill Gates's accomplishments—founder of Microsoft and the largest charitable foundation in the world, named by *Time* as "Person of the Year" in 2005, instrumental in getting a computer on every desk and in most homes—I'm not sure voters would elect him if he ran for office. He has one of the most impressive leadership stories ever achieved in the history of humankind! But if somebody like Bill Gates ran for office, my fellow citizens and the cable news crowd might write him off by saying, "He's too nerdy," "He's too intellectual," "He's not a good public speaker," "He's too quirky."

And that would be our loss.

Luckily, the citizens of Kenilworth, Illinois, did hire the analyzer they needed when they elected Fred Steingraber as president.

Our society is complex. We have complex problems. If we're going to diagnose our problems accurately, I believe we need more great analyzers in government, at the local, state, and federal levels.

Allocating

When Lynn Johnson was appointed as director of Human Services for Jefferson County, Colorado, she knew she faced a challenge with one of her programs. Negative newspaper articles about the inability to deliver food assistance in a timely manner were looming. This was unfortunate, as the department's mission is to help the least fortunate 10 percent of the population gain access to food, shelter, and jobs. Her predecessors had run up large expenses while only achieving some of the desired outcomes, and citizens were being affected.

Lynn immediately went to work. First, she shifted the focus to the customer—the citizen who needed help. The department mantra became "dignity and respect." That simple shift created a positive ripple effect throughout the organization and the community. Dramatic changes were seen in the delivery of services. One destitute woman came into a community services office and was surprised to be greeted with an unusually high degree of respect and professionalism. She later told the government caseworker who helped her, "I have been in and out of government programs for several years. This is the first time somebody asked me if I would like a glass of water and treated me like a person. And I can see a path to taking care of myself now in a way I hadn't seen before. Thank you."

Lynn's next big move was to take a page out of the "lean management" playbook pioneered by Edward Deming. She worked with the agency's leaders to map all of the key processes. "We mapped everything we were doing from the standpoint of the customer and the employee. Our goal was to take out waste. And we wanted to provide better value to the customer. We created a 'stop-doing' list.

"We reduced twenty steps to nine steps. As a result, our staff spends 75 percent of their time with customers now, not 75 percent in low-value-add administrative tasks, as was the case previously."

Finally, Lynn instilled a culture of high performance and continuous improvement. Meetings changed from updates to problem-solving sessions. Reporting was introduced to show where her department was succeeding and failing. Accountability increased. And so did morale of the state employees under her leadership. "Winning is more fun than losing. So once we got our numbers up, our team members were telling me that they never thought this work could be fun, but now they were really having fun being successful."

Under Lynn's direction, the Jefferson County Department of Human Services won a prestigious award for customer service from the U.S. Department of Health and Human Services, which credited the win to a "complete makeover in terms of customer service." When she was asked to comment on the award, Lynn said, "I have the best team of employees who make it all happen; I couldn't do any of it without them."

Isn't that story great? I was so inspired by it that I told it in front of a Colorado House subcommittee hearing on a proposed "lean government" bill (Colorado HB11-1212). I showed up to the hearing expecting bickering and long-windedness, and found exactly that. However, after what seemed like about ten times the time needed to figure out that the bill was worth passing, it was passed after all.

Great leaders, like Lynn Johnson, understand something most people don't. They realize that resources are scarce. Money. Time. Energy. They realize that they can't take the "easy path" of making no–trade-off decisions. Instead, great leaders take the hard and necessary path, focusing on a small set of priorities that matter the most.

Most leaders operate with the same limitations: a set amount of money in the budget, a specific number of people to lead, a certain amount of time to achieve goals. Yet great leaders allocate those resources to their highest and best use, moving them away from areas of waste. And in doing so, they achieve results that others thought impossible.

As governor, John Hickenlooper wanted to replicate his great success in reducing homelessness as mayor of Denver. Roxane White, who had also served as Governor Hickenlooper's mayoral chief of staff, had discovered that it cost the city almost $40,000 annually to have a person homeless, but only $16,000 to get that person into a program and off the streets.

The chronically homeless are almost always what Governor Hickenlooper refers to as "emotionally fragile." They desperately need the framework of a 9-to-5 job and the relationships such a job creates. Even if the compensation only partially covers their living cost, the overall cost to government and society is greatly reduced.

In order to reduce homelessness at the state level, he chose to focus on job creation. More jobs can obviously help reduce homelessness. But more jobs also increase the tax base and provide the revenue needed for social services that help people with medical or substance-abuse problems. "That one factor will have positive spillover effects to help other priorities, either directly or by providing the tax revenue we need," he told me.

Allocating "feels" like deciding. It requires making careful trade-offs, often difficult ones, that may affect vast numbers of people. The work of analyzing leads smoothly into the tough decisions of allocating. Data, evidence, and logic are the foundations of great decisions. Allocating incorporates all of that information—and adds judgment, instincts, and nerve. While it's logical, it's also creative. Getting the most out of the resources under your control often requires a good deal of imagination.

The skill of allocating, if applied poorly, makes a leader seem erratic, or like a slash-and-burn cold-hearted tyrant. But the process of making decisions does not need to be accompanied by yelling or divisive rhetoric. The best leaders say something to the effect of, "Here are the fundamental areas on which we should focus our energy. Here is what we will achieve and by when." Think of the story of Fred Steingraber, and how he calmly laid out the priorities of the village board in his early days as president.

This allocating mode of behavior, if not applied at all, makes a leader appear afraid to make the tough decisions. Little gets accomplished. The status quo reigns. Many elected officials seem reluctant to make decisions. They don't want to upset any constituent group. It takes a great leader to say, "Thank you for your input. This is what we are going to do. This is what we are not going to do. And this is the plan that I believe will improve the quality of life in this community to the greatest extent."

The best allocators are said to be "decisive" or "great prioritizers." They are willing to make tough decisions. They are willing to be innovative, to sometimes break with tradition, to overcome inertia. They are willing to put resources into high-priority new ideas that are likely to produce a large positive impact. They've already done the hard work of analyzing, and they've identified what stakeholders want and need. Now they're ready to make the best plan using the resources at hand and make the investment.

For Governor Rick Snyder of Michigan, smart allocating was simply an extension of sound fiscal responsibility. "I ran as 'one tough nerd'; I am a nerd, and proud of it," he told me, which made me think of him as a strong analyzer. But what he talked about mostly in our interview was shifting the allocation mind-set of the public sector. "One of the first things I found when I came to Lansing, with different groups, is that people would walk into my office, say hello, and ask for money. They would say 'we want money' or 'we need money.' And I would sit there thinking, *So what? Do I look like an ATM?* What I would say to them is, 'I don't care that you want money. You need to walk in here prepared to have a discussion about real results for real people. Talk to me about what outcome or result is going to make a difference in our citizens' lives that's meaningful. Then I'm happy to talk to you about how we prioritize that, how we acquire resources to deliver on it, and how we measure it.' So now people don't walk into my office and ask for money.

"There's a fundamental lack of understanding as to what is good financial practice in the long term," he continued. "There's an undue bias toward short-term cash-in-cash-out. In the public sector, they try to balance the budget in a short-term capacity and they don't really look at the growth of long-term liabilities—pension obligations, post-retiree medical expenses. We have some tough challenges to get through. A lot of these are difficult calls. You have to ask for sacrifices from people. But we have had to push ahead, and now we're seeing some real success." I mentioned in chapter 1 Michigan's recent top-tier economic health rating by Bloomberg.

That's the kind of success more states, more citizens would like to see.

Never has our list of priorities and needs in society seemed so long. And never have our resources seemed so scarce. Great allocators, we need you!

Aligning

Education might be one of the most divisive topics in politics. Approaches and solutions vary from teacher to teacher, school to school, district to district. Efforts to unify priorities within states have met with very mixed results. In some states, critics argue, these efforts have just lead to poorer and poorer outcomes.

But not in Delaware.

In 2010, Delaware was the first state to win the Race to the Top competition, a federal education-reform initiative with high stakes. "We put together a plan that stakeholders across the board had a role in developing," Governor Jack Markell told me. "That included teachers, it included the teachers' union, it included business, it included parents, it included the disability community. We asked people how we could improve education in Delaware. At the end, of course, we had to decide what was going to go in and not go in, but we spent a lot of time listening to other people's ideas and figuring out how to make our plan strongest of all."

The end result of getting everybody unified on a single plan that would affect every school in the state was a federal grant of $119 million. For a state the size of Delaware, that is a significant sum of money.

"I'm a big fan of the line, 'Vision without execution is hallucination,'" said Governor Markell. And the key to execution is aligning.

Great leaders realize that little will get done if they act alone. Once a group's desired outcomes have been identified, once the way to achieve them has been defined and planned, it is time to align. To achieve the desired outcomes, great leaders influence other people to take coordinated action. They understand how a shared mission can galvanize teams and excite customers and stakeholders.

Aligning "feels" like persuading. It is keeping people's sights focused on big-picture goals. Convincing people to do their jobs to the best of their ability. Motivating people to willingly and enthusiastically contribute their talents and energy to achieve results. Simply put, great leaders are persuasive and inclusive, not divisive. (Yet, how many politicians have we put in office who are the opposite?)

Great aligners clarify expectations, they make the case for why tasks are worth doing, and they follow up to make sure those tasks gets done.

This aligning skill, if used to an excessive extent, makes a leader seem "too soft" or look like he "likes to be liked to a fault." Trying to make everybody happy will get you nowhere. This aligning mode, if not used at all, makes a leader seem distant, lacking empathy, or not interested in anybody's opinion but her own. You know the type. The boss who makes big changes without discussing them with anybody, ramming new plans down people's throats. People might go through the motions to execute, but nobody puts in their best effort for leaders who don't care about their teams' opinions.

General Wesley Clark, one of the most decorated military leaders of our time, refers to aligning as "grip." Too tight a grip and people feel smothered. Too little grip and people drift and diffuse their energy, and chaos ensues.

When leaders align well, they are said to be "inspirational" or "consensus-builders." People might commend them on being "firm but fair" in holding others accountable. Leaders with a skill for aligning also communicate well, but be careful! A great aligner is not somebody who just gives feel-good speeches. Today, I evaluate the effectiveness of any speech by the degree to which it motivated me to take action. Don't insult me with rhetoric and vagueness and reflections that assure me that you feel my pain. Instead, influence me to take action! A great aligner can motivate people to act, even when action is hard. Even when they aren't sure whether the leader's plan will succeed.

Ken Griffin is the founder and CEO of Citadel, one of the largest and most successful investment firms in the world. He has grown his company exponentially, partially by attracting the best and brightest in the industry. "When it comes to the hard decisions, the key to success is securing the support of a substantial majority, not just the majority."

Aligning is also about following up on things that need to get done. If you've read the bestseller *The Checklist Manifesto*, you know who author and Harvard surgeon Atul Gawande is. Atul is one of the clearest-thinking and fastest-thinking people I have ever met. It takes him about five minutes to warm up to you upon first meeting. By minute six, his speaking gains momentum, and suddenly you understand why he is such a great aligner. He will tell you his mission in life—to save one million lives. He will leave you with a pause to digest the magnitude of that daunting challenge. Then he will tell you how his checklists are going to achieve it, and you want to help this guy any way you can.

This basic tool of creating and following checklists helps

people make use of existing knowledge they often overlook because they are undisciplined. "It's too simple," some might say. "It's too demeaning." But in 2008, when Dr. Gawande worked with eight hospitals around the globe to implement a simple pre-surgery checklist (including such reminders as "Did you wash your hands?"), thousands of lives were saved. People who would have died, instead lived. That is huge. In fact, major complications dropped 36 percent and deaths as a result of surgery dropped 47 percent.

Dr. Gawande isn't effective at aligning people just because he has the right answers. He is effective because his message is clear and compels others to take action. He has statistics that support his arguments. He has stories that inspire people to do things differently and get the right things done.

Getting things done. Delivering results. Rallying the troops to achieve an objective. These seem absent in many governments today. But if we had more great leaders who align rather than divide in government, the improvement in the performance of government would be astounding for all of us.

• • •

Leadership skills take years of hard work to develop. The 3 As of Leadership are the modes of behavior that great leaders use to achieve the best results. Exploring what great leaders in government were accomplishing through the lens of the 3 As strengthened my belief in the ideas. They are universally applicable. And they offer us a great opportunity to grow as leaders and to identify the strongest leaders in our communities.

That is the "who" approach to government we would be

wise to shift to, since the "what" approach is not working. You cannot legislate great leadership.

You cannot legislate great leadership any more than you can legislate the U.S. Olympic gymnastics team to win gold medals.

High performance is not achieved because of rules and laws and policies. High performance is achieved because great leaders bring people together to achieve a common goal.

Now that we have clarified what we mean by great leadership and have introduced the 3 As of Leadership, let's see in the next chapter what great leaders can achieve in the public sector. And once you turn the page, you will see that I have a secret to share with you.

The Leadocracy Discussion

1. Are great leaders born or made?
2. Which matters more in leadership, "character," "skills," or both equally. Why?
3. As a leader, in which of the 3 As of Leadership are you strongest? And in which "A" would you like to develop your skills further?

CHAPTER 3

Our Most Valuable Untapped Resource

The most dangerous leadership myth is that leaders are born—
that there is a genetic factor to leadership. This myth asserts that
people simply either have certain charismatic qualities or not.
That's nonsense; in fact, the opposite is true.
Leaders are made rather than born.
—Warren G. Bennis

I have a secret to share.

All but one of the government leaders you have been reading about in this book came from the *private* sector.

That's right. The budget-balancing, waste-cutting, performance-enhancing results you are reading about came from private sector leaders who got into government.

Does this start to persuade you that government is not hopeless?

Does it turn on its head the assumption that private sector leaders can't make a difference in government? Are you beginning to think that their leadership skill set might be relevant and transferrable?

Is it becoming clear that we have a valuable, and virtually untapped, resource at our disposal?

The only government leader I feature in this book who grew up exclusively in the public sector is Lynn Johnson. Her story is so great I had to tell you about it. And I wanted to show that I'm not saying *all* government leaders should come out of the private sector. Not at all. There are many great government leaders who built their leadership skills as they worked their way up through the public sector. Abraham Lincoln was one of them. Let's continue to develop great leaders in the public sector.

But what I *am* saying is that we have this huge, virtually untapped resource at our disposal. That resource is the vast number of great leaders in the private sector, who can add tremendously to the great leaders coming up in the public sector.

Great leaders are worth their weight in gold.

What if this country had vast gold reserves that were not being tapped? Reserves that could be used to improve everyone's quality of life? Wouldn't it be smart to find a way to access those reserves and use them?

I believe that the vast pool of private sector leaders in this country are like that unused gold. There are so many amazing leaders in the private sector, but so few of them dare tread into government.

Mark Emkes is a rare private sector leader who got into government. Let's see what he has to say about this experience, the relevance of his private sector leadership skills, and the degree to which he has enjoyed his time in government. Mark began by telling a story of how a private sector sense of urgency was unheard of in his state government when he got there.

Great leaders are worth their weight in gold.

"We know that the federal government is going to cut federal dollars to the state of Tennessee," he said to me. "We don't know when, we don't know how much, we don't know in what areas. But we have to be prepared."

Mr. Emkes is currently serving as Commissioner of Finance and Administration for Tennessee, and his statement surprised me. The idea of contingency planning is not common in government. Mr. Emkes foresaw the likely reduction in federal dollars when the bond rating agencies marked Tennessee's credit ratings for review. At a preliminary meeting in August of 2011, analysts with one rating agency told Mark that they were concerned about the debt ceiling and the discussion of spending cuts in Washington. They expected every state in the union to receive fewer federal dollars at some point. It was hardly a surprise, considering that a supercommittee (which turned out to be not so super) had been formed to trim $1.2 trillion from the federal budget.

How were states going to cope with that?

As Mark told me this story, I wondered the same thing. It sounded terrifying. But he didn't seem rattled as he continued. "We needed to do a hypothetical study. We asked all of the cabinet members and their agencies, 'What would you do if you had to cut 15 percent of your federal dollars? What would you do if you had to cut 30 percent of your federal dollars?'" Every agency contributed. The result was a 153-page report outlining the cuts that would have to be made under the two scenarios. Each agency also identified its greatest funding vulnerabilities, the areas that relied most heavily on federal money.

"We went through that exercise and I sent a letter out about it. The next day, I had the major news affiliates in my office saying, 'What the heck are you doing?' I said, 'Well, we're doing contingency planning. Corporations do this on a monthly basis, sometimes even on a weekly or daily basis, to assess their risk.'"

Mark seemed surprised at their surprise. But this type of urgency, preparation, and risk-mitigating action are standard practices in the private sector. As it turns out, it paid off in the public sector in Mark's case.

When Mark and his team had their next meeting with the rating agencies, the analysts couldn't believe that they had actually performed a risk assessment. "They said that they expect this from corporations but were surprised that we had actually done it." That contingency plan helped cement their top-tier bond ratings—AAA from Moody's and Fitch and AA+ from S&P.

"We were just getting prepared," Mark said. "If and when we get the letter from Washington, D.C., we won't have to panic. We have already thought it through carefully."

Mark brought exceptionally strong leadership skills he honed in the private sector to his government job. This was not his first rodeo. He was familiar with contingency planning and risk assessment. Mark had sharpened his leadership skills for thirty-three years at Bridgestone, the world's largest rubber and tire company. He was so good, they made him CEO of Bridgestone Americas. During his six years as CEO, Mark's leadership delivered record-breaking revenue growth in the mid-2000s. And this is not a popcorn stand. Mark grew his company to achieving $12 billion in revenue with fifty thousand employees, and had achieved environment-friendly LEED certification for his plants across the country. Wow!

Now *that's* a leader!

Twelve billion dollars in revenue. Fifty thousand employees. Award-winning performance over three decades of honing and developing his leadership skills. Contrast Mark's leadership background and results with many of his peers in government who have not really ever led anything. Contrast his background to the backgrounds of bureaucrats who have spent their career sitting on committees and arguing and bickering and not achieving much.

The private sector is a vast resource of leadership talent. It may be our most valuable resource. And for the most part, it is untapped. This resource is renewable. This resource is non-polluting, clean, and, other than producing trace quantities of methane gas, is entirely environmentally friendly. And this resource is virtually unlimited. The only limit is our willingness to tap into it more often.

It's Not New, It's Just Rare

The idea of hiring more private sector leaders into the public sector is not new. I did not invent it. But it is rare.

Guess how many U.S. governors had been successful private sector leaders before getting into government?

Six of fifty. That is only 12 percent!

The rest of the governors either were career politicians, or had tried and failed to be successful in the private sector.

But there are some leaders who are already taking part in the leadocracy movement.

Indiana governor Mitch Daniels is one of those six governors who was a successful private sector leader before becoming leader of a state. He credits his successes as governor to his leadership experiences in the private sector.

Early in his career, he served as Richard Lugar's chief of

staff when Lugar was elected to the Senate in 1976. So he did have some early experience in government. But in 1987 he became president and CEO of an $11 million organization, the Hudson Institute. And in 1990, he accepted a position with Eli Lilly, a highly respected global corporation. He was the president of North American operations from 1993 to 1997, and after achieving great results, was promoted to senior vice president for corporate strategy and policy. Governor Daniels acquired invaluable experience within this large, complex, high-performing organization. Under his leadership, the company doubled its revenue and value, an impressive feat.

In 2001, he jumped from private sector leadership back into government. Leaving Eli Lilly, he became director of the Office of Management and Budget under President George W. Bush. They had presented him with other positions, and he had turned them down. But leading the OMB was the one job he couldn't say no to. After two years with the OMB, Mitch Daniels left and soon after began his campaign for governor.

Another great private sector leader who became governor is Jack Markell of Delaware. He began his career working at First National Bank of Chicago while earning his MBA. He then moved on to the highly respected management consulting firm McKinsey & Company. Then, as the thirteenth employee at Nextel (a name he coined), he helped lead the wireless technology revolution. He served as senior vice president for corporate development before moving on to a senior management position at Comcast.

Where Are the Leaders?

According to the Bureau of Labor Statistics and the Department of Defense, there are approximately 2.28 million leaders in the United States. That means that about 1 percent of the country, or one in every one hundred citizens, holds a position of leadership. That sounds about right. So where is the largest pool of leaders?

By far, the largest pool of leaders is the private sector business community. Seventy-nine percent (1.8 million) of the leaders in this country are in that segment. Military leaders make up 13 percent, or 296,000 leaders. There are approximately 183,000 leaders (8 percent of the total) in the public sector—federal, state, and local government, including government-run schools and hospitals.

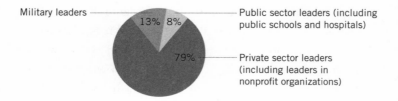

Military leaders — 13% 8% — Public sector leaders (including public schools and hospitals)

79% — Private sector leaders (including leaders in nonprofit organizations)

I'm interested in hiring more great leaders into government. I don't care where they come from. But if you take a "segmented approach" to identifying the biggest source of leaders, you would focus on the private sector, since this is the largest pool.

Thus, this book is geared towards business leaders in the private sector, since they make up over three quarters of the total number of leaders in this country.

So why aren't we seeing more businesspeople in government? We've already discussed one reason—they aren't interested. If only 2 percent of them ever want to go into government, then we are wasting what might be our nation's most valuable natural resource—our great leaders! This is not a problem of making great leaders. It is a problem of finding a way to attract more of them to government service at some point in their careers. One question on the minds of business leaders and voters alike is whether the skills of private sector leaders are relevant to the public sector.

The Skills Are Universally Relevant

Leadership skills are leadership skills.

I have seen nothing to suggest that the 3 As of Leadership are somehow not relevant in the public sector. Sometimes people look at poor leadership in the public sector and say, "That is just how it is in government. The system is bureaucratic." I don't buy that argument anymore. I believe that great leadership skills are universally relevant—that they are useful in any context.

When I was a graduate student working toward my Ph.D. in psychology and leadership, I had an amazing mentor— Peter F. Drucker, who is considered the father of the field of management. For a class project, I observed two different leaders. On one Monday, I went and observed a manager at a government agency, the post office. Then on the next Monday, I went and observed a manager at a Walmart store. The differences in those meetings made an impression on me that has lasted for twenty years.

At the government agency, I noticed that the boss slouched in his chair with his shoulders slumped forward, and talked with a frown on his face. He pointed his finger at the other people in his meeting. The discussion he led was all about rules and compliance—the concerns of bureaucracy—for almost the entire meeting, combined with some unpleasant nagging of the workers. He talked down to them and insulted them.

The boss and the workers complained about customers and how much of a nuisance they were. There was no discussion of problems to be solved, results to be delivered, or accomplishments recently achieved. No mention of analyzing, allocating, or aligning people to achieve great results. But you know what? I didn't fault the government employees themselves. I fault the boss, who was the opposite of a great leader. We can't say, "That's just government. Government is different." No, it isn't! That is just a really poor leader. And poor leadership is poor leadership. And I fault the boss's boss, and the boss's boss's boss, and ultimately, I fault *myself* for being a voter who is responsible for hiring and retaining bureaucrats to manage my postal system, a system that today is on the verge of sputtering out of existence

And I really felt sad for those employees.

They looked miserable.

The Monday after the government meeting, I observed a store manager at Walmart. There, I saw an inspiring display of what is wonderful about great leaders.

For starters, the manager, and everybody at the meeting, was standing up. It was like a pep rally. It was a celebration of a positive, can-do, customer-focused, results-oriented spirit. The store manager led the employees in their song about customers and innovation and reducing waste and improving the customer experience. They hammed it up—there were even butt-wiggles delivered on cue when spelling out W-A-L (butt wiggle) M-A-R-T! They talked numbers. They talked goals and actual results from the previous week. They celebrated wins—one woman named Jen set a record for cash register accuracy and speed and got high-fives from her colleagues, a gift certificate, and a new pin for her blue vest. They were not going through the motions. They were performing and succeeding. There was real-time analyzing, real-time allocating, and real-time aligning. Each one of this team's existence mattered and they knew it.

They looked like they were having fun.

That is the kind of leadership we need in government. And if you ask private sector leaders whether they learned more about leadership during their time in government or during their time in the private sector, they will say private sector. Governor Mitch Daniels told me, "People will sometimes ask, 'Well, geez, you've done different things in your working days. Which ones helped you the most as governor?' They always think I'm going to talk about my OMB experience in Washington, D.C., I never do." He added, "Clearly the much more valuable experiences were those running an $11 or $12 million business or being part of a multibillion-dollar business at Lilly—cost control, getting large numbers of people to move in a common direction, getting the best work out of everybody."

And yet so few of our current governors have had that kind of experience. Only six of fifty governors have had significant leadership success in the private sector before taking office. Twelve percent! That number should be 79 percent (to reflect the proportion of leaders in the private sector). And we wonder why so many states are bankrupt and wasting our taxpayer money every single day.

If 79 percent, not just 12 percent, of our governors came out of the private sector, that would make more sense to me.

Great leaders in the private sector have the full package of skills. They know how to analyze situations, define goals, hire and fire to build great teams, allocate scarce resources toward their highest and best use, reduce waste, hold people accountable to achieving high performance, and deliver great results for customers, employees, and stakeholders.

Simply put, they have become masters of the 3 As of Leadership.

You be the judge. Here are some more success stories I heard, from great private sector leaders who applied their leadership skills in government.

More Success Stories

One of the topics that brought a smile to my face was hearing leaders talk about putting in place better performance measurement, and how unheard of it was in the government organizations they inherited. Governor Daniels bucked resistance and put into place a performance measurement/performance management system. As the saying goes, "What gets managed, gets done." Or, "You can't manage what you don't measure." This is not a "private sector thing" or a "public sector thing"—setting clear goals and measuring performance is a relevant and universal leadership behavior in any context. Did it work in Daniels' state government? You bet it did. Many of the state's agencies, including the Department of Motor Vehicles, the Department of Child Services, and the Department of Corrections, have won national awards. He also spearheaded programs to deliver healthcare coverage to uninsured adults; to revamp the property tax system, resulting in the biggest tax cut in Indiana's history; and to increase land and habitat conservation across the state.

So he must have really run up a big deficit improving the service level of his government, right? Nope. When Mitch Daniels was elected, he inherited a $600 million deficit, which he transformed into a $370 million surplus in one year, without increasing taxes.

Are there other states that would love to swing from a big deficit to a big surplus?

Are there countries that would love to swing from a big deficit to a big surplus?

I think the answer is yes. It's true at the local level, too.

Were his citizens happy with the private sector leadership behaviors he displayed, and the results he and his team achieved? Yes they were!

Governor Daniels was reelected in 2008 with more votes than any candidate in any public office in the state's history.

What struck me is how humble Governor Daniels is. This is not your typical egomaniac, hair perfect, infinite-hot-air politician that we grow weary of seeing on TV. He rarely said "I" during our interview, except when admitting a mistake he made. He said "we" about leadership actions his team made that produced great results. He acted like his actions were not acts of genius, just common sense. And he was proud of the results he reported, not in a boastful or bragging way, but in a way that celebrated the hard work and dedication of his state's leaders and workers. It is like he took a page our of Jim Collins's *Good to Great* concept of a Level 5 leader (humble and disciplined) and lived it every day.

Governor Hickenlooper is cut from similar cloth as Governor Daniels when it comes to leadership competence and humble demeanor. Except John Hickenlooper adds an element of humor to his "I don't take myself too seriously" tone. He ran what was considered the "cleanest" gubernatorial campaign in recent history. For one advertisement, he was videotaped taking a shower while wearing a suit (one of the rare times I've seen him actually wear a tie), saying how he was going to run a clean election. And he did. And he won. And by bringing his private sector leadership skills into the public sector, he is off to an amazing start. I read recently that his popularity numbers put him in the top two of all governors in the country.

And remember Kenilworth president Fred Steingraber? Want to know what he did before serving as mayor of his town? This fellow is possibly the most overqualified government leader I have ever met. He had served as CEO and chairman of A.T. Kearney, the international management consulting firm. Under Fred's leadership, the company achieved massive success. He grew the firm 25 percent per year for eighteen years. Revenue grew from $30 million when he took over to $1.5 billion when he left. Yes, that's billion with a *B*. This created jobs. The number of employees under Fred's leadership grew from two hundred to 6,500. Amazing! Bravo! Imagine all the tax revenue that his firm and the taxpaying employees generated for their countries, states, and municipalities. In addition, he has served on twelve corporate boards, four advisory boards, and over twenty not-for-profit boards.

Were Fred's leadership skills relevant in helping his township balance its budget? Why yes, they were! Within a year of being elected village president, he was able to balance the budget in Kenilworth, Illinois—despite years of deficits. In fact, he is in his third year of a four-year term in which surpluses continue and increase each year.

This reminds me, jobs are important. And who better to attract or create revenue-generating jobs (that is what governors call "tax paying" as opposed to "tax spending") than someone who had created jobs before? It is hard to create jobs. Really hard.

After he was elected governor of Delaware but before he was sworn in, Jack Markell received some bad news. He knew that job creation was a top priority. So you can imagine how disappointed he was when both Chrysler and General Motors decided to close their manufacturing plants in his state. And then oil company Valero decided to close its refinery. "Those three employers represented by far the best opportunities for high school graduates in Delaware to enter the middle class over the coming decades. So that was a kick in the gut."

How did Governor Markell respond to this crisis? He showed that he understood what matters to the companies that would bring more jobs into his state.

"I'm convinced that one of the most important things people in my role have to do is to put ourselves into the shoes of people who create jobs and focus in on the things they care the most about. They want to be in communities with very good schools, reasonable taxes, a great work force, a great quality of life, and a really responsive government.

"Two and half years later, the General Motors plant has been purchased by Fisker Automotive. They're going to be making a really gorgeous plug-in hybrid car starting the end of next year. They've already started to hire. The Chrysler plant has been purchased by the University of Delaware—they're building a new science and technology campus—and a company called Bloom energy—they make fuel cells for major companies. And the refinery has also reopened. These companies had lots of choices about where they could locate their new facilities. They chose Delaware. If you were to talk to the leaders of those companies they would tell you it's because Delaware gets it. We're responsive, we think like they do, we know that as long as companies are filling out forms and waiting in line they're not putting people to work."

I recognize that not every leader in the private sector is strong enough to perform well in the public sector. But our very best leaders in the private sector have the full package of leadership skills we need. The problems we are facing in society and in government are too complex for the B (bureaucracy) team. We need the A team in there—masters of the 3 As of Leadership.

New York City mayor Michael Bloomberg has a saying: "Everybody always says 'What's the difference between business and government?' And I always joke, one's a dog-eat-dog world and the other's the reverse."[5] Business is hard. Government is hard. The right leaders can save the day in both situations.

Even More Success Stories

Fellow citizens, there are a few more stories I think you will enjoy about private sector leaders doing great things in the public sector. One of the keys to making the leadocracy movement grow is to persuade my fellow citizens, beyond a reasonable doubt, that we want private sector leaders to go into government.

There is this bias out there that private sector leaders who go into government are egomaniacal, corrupt jerks. There is a kernel of truth in that: some are. But you just have to sift out the bad ones and hire the great ones. And those egomaniacal, corrupt ones? They were never good leaders to begin with!

As I have been discussing the concept of leadocracy with people I respect in the business community, several have pointed me in the direction of high integrity, non-corrupt leaders in government who came from the private sector. That's how I came to talk with Mark Emkes. When I presented my ideas to Joe Scarlett of the Scarlett Leadership Institute (and former CEO of the wildly successful Tractor Supply Company), he said, "You should really talk to Mark Emkes. He cannot be corrupted, he only has the best interest of the state at heart, he doesn't give a damn about getting ahead, he's untouchable in terms of influence, and he's just making good financial decisions for the state because he has no other motivation."

You may be thinking that private sector leaders in government may allocate resources directly into the hands of friends and former companies. That's happened, sure. You may be thinking that business leaders are heartless, corrupt. Sometimes that's true. But those people aren't great, 3-A leaders. They weren't leaders at all.

Take Bernie Madoff, Bernie Ebbers of WorldCom, or Jeff Skilling of Enron. Were they great leaders? No. They rose to power, yes, and they temporarily produced attractive returns for their investors. But they were convicted of committing fraud. And it is not clear that they wanted to achieve anything else in life other than making money. But all businesspeople are not like that.

Compare them with another type of leader, those like Governor Rick Snyder of Michigan. At a young age, he decided that he wanted his career to go in stages. First, he wanted to build a career in the private sector, where he could learn valuable skills and make money. They he wanted to have a stage of his career in the public sector so that he could serve his community. The final stage of his projected career is to be a teacher. So he earned a CPA, an MBA, and a JD, all by the age of twenty-four. In the private sector, he performed at the highest level at Coopers & Lybrand (now PriceWaterhouseCoopers) and made partner in only six years. He then helped grow Gateway, the computer company, from seven hundred employees to ten thousand. Along the way, they took the company public. When it became a large organization, he followed his entrepreneurial spirit and formed his own venture capital firm and has helped create jobs and built companies in a variety of industries. Now, he serves as governor, leveraging his experience and making tough decisions for the state of Michigan, balancing the budget and serving the citizens in a variety of ways.

• • •

Without great leaders, government will not self-correct its trajectory of bureaucracy. "Government is the last monopoly," Mitch Daniels said to me. "I always say there's a reason we don't trust monopolies in America. They overcharge and underserve their customers. There's no competition to make them do otherwise. So you either implant accountability into government or it's not going to be there. Businesspeople get that."

If the citizens of the United States had hired my firm to do leadership succession in our fifty states, I guarantee you that we would not have selected the current roster of governors. Imagine how much we could get done with more John Hickenloopers, Jack Markells, Rick Snyders, and Mitch Danielses in office across the country.

We could expect more balanced budgets, a safer and stronger platform for job creation, and a better quality of life. That is what you get with more great leaders in government. That is what you get when more leaders practice the 3 As of Leadership to effectively analyze what their citizens need, allocate scarce resources to their highest and best use, and align people to take collective action to achieve the desired outcomes.

Has this chapter persuaded you that great private sector leaders are out there, a vast untapped resource at our disposal? Do you want more of these masters of the 3 As of Leadership in office? I do.

But there is one problem. Remember when Governor Hickenlooper told me, "They won't come"? Our next order of business becomes answering the question, "How do we get our greatest leaders to *want* to go into government?" This begins with identifying the reasons why they avoid government, which is the subject of the next chapter.

The Leadocracy Discussion

1. Do you think that leadership skills are universally relevant?
2. To what extent do you want to tap more leaders from the private sector and see them in government?
3. What would happen if we ran our governments like we run the highest-performing companies in our country?

CHAPTER 4

Why Great Leaders
Avoid Government

*Woodrow Wilson called for leaders who, by boldly interpreting
the nation's conscience, could lift a people out of
their everyday selves. That people can be lifted into their better
selves is the secret of transforming leadership.*
—*James MacGregor Burns*

If you are an accomplished private sector leader, please stick
with me.

I chose to invest the first half of this book in persuading
my fellow voting populace of something you already know—
that society would benefit if we had more great private sector
leaders like you in government.

Now, please allow me to try to persuade *you* to go into
government.

I'm going to do that by first reflecting on my understanding of why you avoid government.

Maybe you are like Joe Scarlett. His private sector leadership story is impressive. Soon after Joe was hired as a vice
president with Tractor Supply Company, he found out that

the business was losing money. A lot of money. Eighteen months later, the parent company fired the CEO and brought in a temporary caretaker to try to salvage the retail chain.

"It looked like we were going to go down the drain," Joe told me. A sad ending for a company founded in 1938, with a proud heritage and a valuable service to farmers.

But then something happened. The parent company made the caretaker the new president, and he made Joe his number two. Together, they began a transformation.

"We went from losing thirteen million to losing five million the next year to breaking even the next year to making a profit ever since." That was in the early 1980s. How did they achieve this turnaround?

First, when the parent company put Tractor Supply up for sale, the new CEO, Joe, and three other leaders in the company put together a leveraged buyout. Second, they identified a new core customer called the "hobby farmer." And they worked to meet that customer's needs through their locations, the products they sold, their hours of operation, and so on.

But neither of those was the most important element of success, according to Joe. It was all about talent and culture. "We built a very powerful culture based on always doing the right things, taking an extraordinary amount of time to hire the best people, and creating an educational network to make sure that those people were fully qualified to run stores and distribution centers."

They invested heavily in creating an ethical, high-performance organization. Joe eventually became CEO of Tractor Supply and held that position for more than ten years. He took the company public, quadrupled revenue, and grew the stock price *tenfold*. Tractor Supply was honored by *Forbes* as one of the "Best Managed Companies in America." When he retired from Tractor Supply in 2007, Joe and his family founded the Scarlett Leadership Institute to provide ethical leadership education to students of all ages.

Joe's story of what he achieved and how he achieved it made me want to hire him into government. I could see clearly how he might turn around a struggling agency the same way he turned around Tractor Supply: by hiring strong talent, by better meeting the needs of customers, by creating a culture based on ethics, by running a tight ship, and by building a high-performance organization. So I asked him a provocative question.

"Would you ever consider a job in government leadership?"

He replied, "You know, I think to myself, I would love to *be* president of the United States, but I wouldn't want to do what it takes to get there. I'm probably not interested in going into government at this stage of the game." He added that government has always been unfamiliar to him, a sector he did not dare tread into.

Joe Scarlett is the type of leader any of us would want to see in government. But we can't get him. We can't get a lot of people like him.

Months ago, I started asking the best leaders I know that same question—"Would you ever consider a job in government leadership?" I expected their answers to be some version of "No way! Are you nuts?"

I was right.

I hear you, I thought as I listened to their objections. I had felt the same way about the idea. But I wanted to get to the *why*. If we could only identify the common obstacles preventing great leaders from going into government, perhaps we could remove them.

Based on some early conversations, I thought I understood the objections most leaders would raise. They were similar to my own. But as I talked to more leaders, they expressed some other concerns that surprised me. The three obstacles they most often cited were:

1. **Confidence.** Leaders lack confidence in their knowledge of government and in the bureaucratic system. They said, "I won't be able to get anything done because I don't have the knowledge base and because of all the bureaucracy."

2. **Cost.** Leaders think the required sacrifices might be too great. "I'm not willing to suffer the financial cost or the psychological cost of playing the political game," they told me.

3. **Confidentiality.** Leaders are afraid of media exposure. Time and again, I heard, "I don't want to subject my family or myself to the public scrutiny."

Let's explore these obstacles, first from the private sector leader's perspective. Then let's ask some public sector leaders what the reality is.

Obstacle 1 = Confidence

Most great leaders only take jobs in which they are confident they can succeed.

And many are so unfamiliar with government. But what they know understandably scares them and makes them question whether they could succeed. In government, they see too many risks and too few opportunities. The two biggest hits to their confidence are their own lack of knowledge and experience in government and their fear that the massive bureaucracy would prevent them from applying their talents in a way that makes a difference.

"My first reaction was, 'I'm not qualified.'" Kristin Russell told me this as she explained why she initially decided against taking the position of secretary of technology and chief information officer for the state of Colorado. The world of government was so foreign to her. She described her lack of understanding with big gestures, smiling broadly. Kristin, by the way, does not act like any information technology person or government leader I have ever met. She is full-energy, full-charisma, and is not afraid to speak her mind, regardless of the situation. Her personality reminds me of Leigh Anne Tuohy, the sharp-tongued woman with a heart of gold played by Sandra Bullock in *The Blind Side*. "They said, 'Kristin, you'll sit on the governor's cabinet,' and I thought, I don't even know what that means. So my first reaction was, 'That's very nice, but no. I can't do this. I don't have the skills, I don't understand government, and I don't want to do this.'"

Luckily for the citizens of Colorado, Kristin eventually changed her mind. When I talked with her for this book, she had been on the job about a year. It had taken her about six months to get up to speed. Six months. That did not seem too bad. Kristin had been vice president of global IT service operations with Oracle, responsible for all data centers and computing operations worldwide. She rose to a similar position with Sun Microsystems before that. I asked her how long it had taken her to get up to speed in her previous leadership positions in the private sector. "Actually, the same amount of time. About six months," she said. Six months to get up to speed in the private sector, six months to get up to speed in the government leadership job.

Getting up to speed in a government role is easier than in the private sector, in some respects, Kristin Russell pointed out. "There's a ton of documentation available in government, whereas in the private sector it's a lot more folkloric, passing the information from person to person."

That doesn't help solve the problem of bureaucracy and lack of authority, though.

Iced tea nearly sprayed out of Tyler Tysdal's nose when I asked, "Would you ever consider a job in government leadership?" He started to laugh and then choked on his drink.

When he finally stopped choking and could speak again, he said, "Government? Uh, no." Then he resumed digging into his chicken Caesar salad.

Tyler is an amazing leader. He grew up in the rural plains of Nebraska. An upbringing of honest hard work helped develop his natural leadership skills. He served as student council president in high school and at Georgetown University, worked as an intern in Washington, D.C., for Congresswoman Virginia Smith, earned an MBA from Harvard Business School, and then founded, led, or invested in about a dozen successful companies during his impressive career.

"Tell me why you wouldn't do it," I said.

Tyler took a deep breath, thought for a moment, and replied, "Mostly it's because I wouldn't be able to use my skills. Politics is all about . . . well . . . politicking. My sense is that you're restricted from really getting things done. You have to constantly follow rules and policies and operate within a vast bureaucracy, all of which limit your authority. You aren't free to just lead. That sounds horribly frustrating to me given my successes in business. No way, I'm not interested in politics anymore."

Ted Waitt, founder of Gateway, captured the sentiment well after I asked him the question. "Would you ever consider a job in government leadership?" He said no. I asked why. He said, "In most political jobs, you have your ass on the line and you can't make a difference." That was a pretty common and understandable response.

"My perception is that most government organizations are slow moving," Aaron Kennedy said. Aaron is the founder of Noodles & Company, one of the great entrepreneurial success stories of Colorado. Aaron might remind you of a marketing executive from Pepsi, because he was a marketing executive with Pepsi before he became an entrepreneur. He has a boyish but responsible face, stylish glasses, an easy smile, a command of language and numbers, and a strong sense of brand. He founded the Noodles & Company chain with his first restaurant in 1995. It has grown to become a national franchise of more than 284 restaurants. Noodles & Company brings in over $300 million in revenue and employs over 7,000 people.

Aaron is an amazing leader. Harvard Business School wrote a case study on him that is today taught to all nine hundred first-year MBA students. Aaron was also named "Entrepreneur of the Year" by Ernst & Young in 2011. Noodles & Company has won multiple awards, including being named one of America's "Top 10 Healthiest Fast Food Restaurants" by *Health* magazine and one of the "10 Best Family Restaurants" by *Parents* magazine. After he retired from his CEO position, he worked on his own farm and founded Commotion Fresh Foods, a company devoted to providing kids' food that's healthy, delicious, nutritious, and easy and affordable for mom and dad. He is the type of talented, high-integrity leader who would be effective in any environment, including government.

But Aaron wasn't so sure. "These organizations are fraught with what bureaucracy means in most people's minds. So it's a very difficult infrastructure and set of rules to navigate. They would be barriers to your success."

The issue of bureaucracy is a real one. I said so myself in the introduction. But what I discovered by talking with business leaders who serve in government is that you actually can make a difference in government *if you choose to do so*. It's possible to overcome the negative inertia of bureaucracy. It just takes a leader who has vision beyond the obstacle, who is focused, and who is driven to take action.

When I asked Governor Mitch Daniels about this obstacle, his first thought was of the civil service unions representing Indiana state employees and making the bureaucracy worse. The union contracts were crippling the government's ability to make organizational changes that would improve efficiency and effectiveness. "We got rid of 160 pages of collective-bargaining agreements that would have really hamstrung progress. I don't know if I could have kept some of the people who came with us if we hadn't taken these handcuffs off our leaders." As Governor Daniels described in his book, *Keeping the Republic* (Sentinel, 2011), "The agreements were so specific and dense that, under their stipulations, we could barely move a photocopier without union permission. As for paying the best workers more, moving the worst workers out, reorganizing departments, or outsourcing services to private companies, that was simply impossible." And the agreements mandated that the state collect about 2 percent of every state employee's salary, whether they liked it or not.

So what did Governor Daniels do? Wring his hands with worry about how little authority he had to make things happen? Nope. On his second day in office, he signed an executive order ending Indiana's compulsory unionism for state employees. Boom. Bye bye bureaucracy. And though he expected protests and outraged op-eds, it never happened. Public servants took it in stride. Eventually, free to make their own choices, 90 percent of them stopped paying union dues.

That one crucial move allowed his appointed leaders to quickly and effectively make vast leadership changes to poorly performing departments. When Governor Daniels entered office in 2004, Indiana had one of the worst child welfare systems in the country. By 2011, the reorganized, revamped, and reenergized Indiana Department of Child Services had won national awards, was a model for other states, and was serving the children of Indiana on a whole new level.

Taking on the bureaucracy, he found, was not impossible. And he was surprised how much he was able to achieve as governor. I asked him point-blank whether this job has been satisfying or not. Governor Daniels said, "For me, this job has been a positive surprise. There's plenty of what we call gridlock all over American politics. I didn't know how much of what we wanted to do we could actually get done. But we have gotten an awful lot of things done. More than I might have hoped at the outset. I was introduced last night by a political columnist to a bunch of newspaper editors. He said, 'We've had more change and more action to cover in the last seven years than in the previous seven generations.'"

When I asked Governor Hickenlooper whether it is possible to break through bureaucracy and make a difference in government, he said, "Yes, you can. It's not as direct as in the private sector, where you just decide something. You have the extra step of convincing the legislature. But that is not much different from making a decision and having to convince your board or your key executives to put it into action."

Something Kristin Russell said floored me. "When you're in these government leadership roles, there's an immediate authority that comes along with them," she said. Amazingly, she actually feels just the opposite of what private sector leaders fear—she said she has *more* authority and control in her government job than in her previous private sector jobs. She said, "Even at very senior-level positions in the private sector, you don't have the scope and authority that you have in these government leadership positions. The authority and autonomy I have here at the state is totally energizing."

Bottom line: one reason that private sector leaders avoid government is that they don't have the confidence that they will be able to have authority and succeed in that environment. However, the private sector leaders who actually made the leap into government tell me the opposite—that they have found that they have plenty of authority and opportunity to make a difference. This leads me to conclude that obstacle number one, confidence, comes more from a lack of familiarity than from a true structural barrier preventing leaders from being successful in government. Great leaders can make decisions in government. They can reduce bureaucracy. They can power through the remaining bureaucratic obstacles to get things done and be successful in that context.

Obstacle 2 = Cost

Darrin Anderson is the type of leader anybody would love to have in government. His talent is matched by his rock-solid character. And for all of the hardships and challenges he has overcome in his life, you might expect him to be serious and reserved. But he is a teddy bear of a man, with an easy laugh and a preacher's southern drawl that is full of positivity. For anybody who thinks business leaders are all blue-blooded members of the aristocracy and that the American Dream is dead, consider Darrin's story.

Darrin grew up in rural Illinois in a family that struggled to make ends meet. His father worked two jobs. His mother stayed home with Darrin and his three younger siblings. To make their grocery money go as far as possible, his mother served "wilk"—watered down milk—at breakfast.

Darrin began developing his leadership skills early. He was MVP of his high school football team and captain of both his football and basketball teams. He graduated from the United States Military Academy at West Point with a B.S. in economics, commanded a scout platoon for a tank division in Desert Storm, and earned a Bronze Star. When he left the U.S. Army, he was highest ranked out of thirty first lieutenants in his peer group.

Darrin then entered the private sector and rose quickly through the ranks of various companies because of his A-level performance. As a surgical equipment rep, he grew revenue for his company by 400 percent. At Alliant Food-service, he took the worst-performing business unit and its negative $500,000 EBITDA and grew it to $2 million in EBITDA in two years. Today, as regional vice president for HD Supply, he regularly surpasses metrics and goals, and his team members have called the CEO to extol Darrin's virtues as the best boss they've ever had. It seems that everywhere he goes, he increases revenue, reduces costs, turns failing departments and divisions around, and improves the performance and morale of his teams.

I was talking with Darrin recently when I hijacked the conversation and asked, "Would you ever consider a job in government leadership?"

He replied without hesitation. "No."

For Darrin, the primary obstacle was cost: First, the opportunity cost of lost income because of the higher salary he can earn in the private sector and the potential long-term effects of leaving his career track. Second, the cost to his psyche of playing politics.

Darrin didn't grow up rich, remember. And he is right in the prime earning potential of his career. He wants to provide a safe, comfortable home and college educations for his children. "Getting off the private sector track to work in government could be extremely costly to me and my family. I'm not willing to make that sacrifice."

Kristin Russell's take on the career cost of service was slightly different. She feared that she'd have to give up her private sector life entirely! "My biggest fear was that I was going to take this pretty big risk and then I would have to stay in government for the rest of my life. I wouldn't be able to exit, to get back to the private sector. My skills weren't going to be relevant. Or I'd be kind of tainted under this umbrella of like, you're a public sector employee, you don't really get it, you've been disassociated with the real world."

It's true that many talented public servants can't achieve the same level of income that they might be able to in the private sector. Government has to run on a tight budget, always. But if you already have a strong career in the private sector, the cost doesn't have to be that great. You can do a lot of work and achieve great results in just a couple of years.

Two years of reduced income is not going to matter much over one's lifetime, particularly for leaders of high caliber.

Assume you work from age twenty to age sixty-five. That is forty-five years. If you do a stint in government along the way for two years, that is only 4 percent of your career at reduced earning potential.

A short stint in government also isn't likely to hurt your career trajectory or make you undesirable. Quite the contrary. Kristin Russell had people who supported her move into government and promised her an exit strategy when her term is done. It's easier in this country than in many others to move in and out of public service with little danger of sacrificing career growth. You don't have to opt into public service at an early age and make a life of it. Many people leave the public sector and have successful private sector lives.

Brian Selander is chief strategy officer for Governor Markell, and is a talented, mid-career professional who has worked in both the private and public sectors. He told me, "I found that time in government did (and will) make me a better leader in business. Having to mobilize or inspire teams without the benefit of financial incentives, having to walk the high wire of daily media scrutiny, having competitors focused not just on taking market share but on actually taking you out of circulation, having to boil complex policy arguments down into a few seconds compelling enough to break through the clutter and move public perception—it can be a crucible you don't always find in business."

It is possible to pay "market wages" for top talent in government, but rarely. The best leaders in positions to make a difference recognize the challenges to getting more great leaders into government. They are finding ways to break down these obstacles. Governor Mitch Daniels abolished the state's Department of Commerce and created the Economic Development Corporation, a public-private nonprofit corporation instead. And because it received public funds but also private money, it could afford to attract top-tier talent to the problem of improving the economic environment in Indiana. "Sometimes you need to pay a little more than government scale to get these people," Governor Daniels explained. Over time, more private-public partnerships could help increase the benefits of public service.

And Governor John Hickenlooper is developing plans for what *The Denver Post* called "the most sweeping changes in forty years to the state's personnel system."[6] His goal? To break down the rigid regulations that make it difficult for government leaders to attract and reward the most talented employees.

Beyond the financial and career costs, leaders fear the psychological cost of politicking. Darrin Anderson couldn't wrap his mind around the more odious responsibilities of government officials: "There are these factions you have to please. Cut costs but don't touch the benefits for the elderly! Don't anger the unions. Kissing butts and pandering to so many groups just to get the job and keep the job. That's just not how I want to spend my time."

As Joe Scarlett talked about the much-admired governor of Tennessee, Bill Haslam, he mirrored Darrin's sentiment. "What he had to do to become governor is something that very few businesspeople would ever do. He spent the better part of two years all over Tennessee, going to one fundraiser after another. He was selling himself. He was shaking hands and kissing babies, as they say. And it's just a debilitating thing to have to do. I would never do that. And most leaders would not."

As I heard similar concerns from other leaders, I realized that they were primarily talking about the process of getting *elected*. Yet in federal, state, and local governments, the percentage of people in leadership positions, not including legislators, who are elected is actually quite small.

Most leadership positions in government are appointed or hired. I think a reasonable first job in government for a private sector leader is in an appointed role, not an elected one.

When Mark Emkes got the call from Governor-elect Bill Haslam to be commissioner of finance and administration, he said, "I'm not sure I'm the right guy, 'cause I've been talking bad about government all my life." Governor Haslam responded, "So have I. What other problems do you have?" For Mark, that gave the governor instant credibility.

To wrap up obstacle number two, cost, let's just say that yes, there is cost to serving in government. However, if you only do a short stint, that cost is invisible to the naked eye across your career. And the psychological cost is likely to be small, too, if you pursue an appointed role in the executive branch. It's likely to be more costly in terms of money and anguish if you pursue an elected role, because of the campaigning required.

Obstacle 3 = Confidentiality

"A lot of great leaders are private people," Tom Hill told me recently. Tom is vice chairman at the Blackstone Group and was previously the CEO of a global company. "They aren't willing to endure the public scrutiny and meddling in their private life, releasing personal financial information, their stock and real estate holdings, etc."

Mike Fries had a similar concern. He helped build Liberty Global, an international cable TV company, from nearly scratch to $10 billion in revenue. Liberty now has operations in fourteen countries, serves 18 million customers, and employs over twenty thousand people. Mike is a no-nonsense guy of quick movements, with the jaw of a young Robert De Niro. I know Mike through the Young Presidents' Organization; he is considered to be one of the most talented and successful members in the history of our chapter. I asked Mike whether he would consider a job in government, and he said that while he's thought about it, two issues usually arise. "First, by the time I retire from the private sector, I might be able to make a greater impact through my foundation or not-for-profits. Government? I don't know. I worry about putting my family through that."

Andreas Bauer, a partner who leads a professional-services firm in Austria, confirmed Tom's take. "Yeah. The scrutiny is a problem. I don't want the world to know who I choose to have lunch with, and all the controversy I would fear around my comings and goings."

For Aaron Kennedy, founder of Noodles & Company, the invasion into his personal life was the biggest concern. "Maybe I have too thin of a skin. I don't have skeletons in my closet, but it just seems like it is so brutal today with the press and the Internet and bloggers. What would my kids be exposed to if I ran for an elected position? To me it just seems excruciatingly painful for spouses and children."

That was the biggest obstacle for Governor Jack Markell before he decided to run for election, too. "Numbers 1, 2, and 3 on the negatives list was the idea of my wife, my mom, my kids reading nasty letters to the editor and hearing nasty things.

But my kids really helped me a lot once I started thinking more about running for governor. My wife asked them, 'What would your reaction be if kids at school said nasty things about your dad?' And they said, 'We know who our dad is.' To me that was a very reaffirming statement. You know, people are going to say things that aren't very flattering. Some may be true; some may not be true. But in the end, all I can live with is whether or not I've done my very best."

Government leaders work for us. They work for the citizens. Citizens have a right to know important details about the leaders they are considering for government leadership, and about those placed into leadership positions by elected officials. This scrutiny can be uncomfortable for leaders. But Earl Goode, Mitch Daniels's chief of staff, said it best: "If you do the ethical, honest, and right thing, you have nothing to hide."

Alternatively, if you choose to take a photograph of your private parts and send it to your constituents, you're going to receive a high level of scrutiny. But if you're honest, ethical, and do good work, the type and level of scrutiny you'll receive will be vastly different. And that's the case for 99 percent of public sector leaders.

Sure, there is the Freedom of Information Act, which makes emails and letter correspondence of government officials public record. All members of an administration will be under scrutiny from the press and from the opposition. Only twice or three times across the past year of advising the governor of Colorado did I hear staffers make any comments about confidentiality concerns. Most of the government leaders I spoke with told me that these facts of life weren't much of an issue. Earl Goode said that two people on Governor Daniels's staff had done something inappropriate, and the first time the press heard about either incident was when those people were fired.

Mark Emkes had to disclose all of his *sources* of income, but not the *amounts*. Why was that important to him? "My kids think I'm poor and I want to keep it that way." Ha!

Kristin Russell has been able to maintain her personal leadership style and leverage it to build trust with her team. "I'm very open. I'm very direct. I'll swear occasionally. I'll say things that are on my mind. And I haven't stopped doing that. I know that I'm going to get my ass chewed about it one of these days, but it's who I am, it's part of my brand, and I'm not willing to sacrifice that regardless of the personal stakes." So far, she hasn't had to make that sacrifice. "I'm going to continue to be open and pragmatic, and if that means my words get twisted sometimes, so be it." For her, the issue of scrutiny has not been much of an issue at all.

For great leaders, transparency isn't a problem. In fact, public discussion of your work can be an accelerator, a way to get the message out.

Mitch Daniels invites scrutiny of his administration's results in Indiana, and Fred Steingraber does the same in Kenilworth, Illinois. They use newsletters, reports, and the Internet to share as much information as possible. Rick Snyder, the CPA/MBA governor, posts his administration's goals and results for everyone to see. Imagine that.

Yes, there may be interest groups who don't like you. Yes, there may be reporters who bother you occasionally. Depending upon your position, you may need to disclose some details of your personal finances. But unless you are the president of a country, the amount of scrutiny and intrusiveness you will actually feel is minimal in a government leadership role. In fact,

these days, I see CEOs of public companies suffering more public scrutiny than, say, the director of human services for a state.

• • •

These three obstacles are real in the minds of great leaders.
Great private sector leaders worry about having the confidence to be successful in government, they worry about cost,
and they worry about confidentiality. However, I'm here to tell
you that the leaders who actually made the leap into government don't think these issues are very big once they get there.

And I discovered the "antidote" to these three Cs that prevent great leaders from getting into government. It is also a C.
Choice.

To maximize your effectiveness and reduce the confidence
obstacle, *choose* to assert the authority you do have, and choose
to remove structural impediments to progress! To reduce the
cost obstacle, *choose* to limit your service in government to
two years and take a cabinet role rather than an elective role
(which requires more time and money). To reduce the scrutiny
obstacle, *choose* to keep your private parts in your pants and use
the media as a vehicle to get your message out.

Hear that, great leaders? The concerns you have are valid,
but the reality is not as bad as you think it is. So let's get the
word out to our best leaders and demystify these obstacles. If
somebody had done that for Joe Scarlett, he might have been
willing to do a stint in government. "I just have never understood government. I just don't know about it. If you had given
me some opportunities to ask questions and brainstorm about
the topic ten years ago, so that I could get familiar with what
it really takes. If you would have said, 'Hey Joe, we're going to

have a couple of workshops for people who might be interested in getting into government, would you be interested in learning about it?' My answer would have probably been yes."

Let's work to remove these obstacles so that more great leaders like Joe Scarlett can step into government. We'll find ways to make it happen if we really want our quality of life to continue to improve.

So are you still with me, great leaders? If so, I imagine you might be thinking, "OK, so you just told me that the downside of being in government is not as bad as I might fear. So what's the upside?" To find out, please turn the page. In the next chapter, we will explore the reality of the benefits you get from serving in government.

The Leadocracy Discussion

1. What prevents you from going into government?
2. What can be done to educate great leaders about government, to boost their confidence that they can be successful?
3. How might we reduce the costs to great leaders for serving in elective or appointed government leadership roles?
4. As voters and consumers of media, we put candidates though an unpleasant and ineffective selection process (e.g., sensationalism, theatrical debates, sound bites, reputation brutality, etc.). To what extent does this scare off our very best leaders from choosing to run or serve? How might we improve the leader-selection process and make it more substantive and less ridiculous?

CHAPTER 5

What's in It for You

Most enjoyable activities are not natural;
they demand an effort that initially one is reluctant to make.
—*Mihaly Csikszentmihalyi,* Flow: The Psychology of
Optimal Experience

What is it actually like to be in government?

Is it a great experience? Or is it usually a lousy one? I did not know. So I asked leaders who had made the leap from the private sector into the public sector. What I learned surprised me. What were possible answers I expected to hear?

- Hypothesis #1: Government service is nothing but painful.
- Hypothesis #2: Government service is merely worthwhile.
- Hypothesis #3: Government service is a great leadership adventure.

I found evidence that supports hypothesis #3. Most leaders I talked with and worked with described their time in government as a great leadership adventure.

When I asked these leaders how they enjoyed their stint in government, the most common answer was some version of "My time in government leadership has been the most rewarding professional experience of my life." Wow. That is not what I expected when I began this journey.

Now, I did not do a formal survey of thousands of people. I don't know the degree to which my findings along this journey represent the experiences of all leaders who have ever crossed over from the private sector to work in the public sector. I would encourage universities and non-partisan think tanks to undertake large research projects to test some of the findings in this book. It would be great to see what they find with larger sample sizes, across more geographies, and across the various levels of local, state, and federal government.

The method I used was talking with the handful of people I was aware of who made the leap into government. I simply asked them what they found when they got there, what they achieved, and how they liked it.

As I heard leader after leader telling me that they really enjoyed their time in government, my next question was, *Why?* These are people who had amazing careers at the top of the private sector leadership food chain. They led massive organizations with global brands. They used their talent to successfully grow these companies. They delighted customers, provided jobs for employees, and earned attractive returns for their investors. So why were they raving about their government leadership experience?

What is so great about working in government?

To shed light on this question, I sought counsel from three sources: leaders who had not yet made the leap into government, leaders who had already made the leap, and the world expert in job satisfaction.

When I talked to Aaron Kennedy, founder of Noodles & Company, about the possibility of serving in government, he touched on what may be an unmet need in successful private sector leaders. "I feel like there is something else I should be doing, but I can't find it. I think there are a lot of people like me. We want something that really makes use of our leadership skills in a way that is challenging but worthwhile."

The need that Aaron was describing reminded me of the concept of "flow." Flow is the highest state of work satisfaction. You know when you are using your skills to their highest level, focusing on a worthwhile task that has a high degree of challenge, and you lose yourself in the task because it is so enjoyable? That is flow. Flow happens when a great sales executive is in the middle of closing a big deal. It happens when a brilliant software developer is coding a blockbuster program, completely engrossed in the task at hand. It happens when a leader is in the process of applying the 3 As of Leadership and sees the excitement on the faces of key constituents.

Flow is in the domain of "positive psychology." The grandfather of this domain and the leading expert on flow is Mihaly Csikszentmihalyi. He asks you to call him Mike. Mike coined the term *flow* in his bestselling book *Flow: The Psychology of Optimal Experience*. He is a professor in the Peter F. Drucker and Masatoshi Ito Graduate School of Management at Claremont Graduate University near Los Angeles, which is where I earned my Ph.D. So I gave him a call, and he was nice enough to take it. As I picked his brain on this topic, I asked him to help me make sense of what I was hearing from the leaders. "What about your notion of 'flow' might explain why private sector leaders rave about their time in government leadership?" I asked.

He said, "Our culture has become more and more special-ized, and more and more bureaucratic in many ways. Who we are gets constricted by the demands of more specialized jobs. The parts of ourselves that we can express, that we can use in the average job—they are only a small part of who we are and what we can accomplish. Every time we use a strength, we enjoy it. Those who have succeeded in their careers now can divert some of their energy. They are looking to expand their growth potential and experience flow. They feel that they have things to contribute. They want an opportunity for expressing some strength they have that is not used."

That makes sense. Great leaders love to lead! Holding on to a corporate job that has become routine does not offer many chances to experience flow. Neither does being retired. Because flow is "the state in which people are so involved in an activity that nothing else seems to matter; the experience itself is so enjoyable that people will do it even at great cost, for the sheer sake of doing it."[7] There are two critical characteristics of activities that induce this state of flow. First, the activities offer challenges that require the use of old skills and the learning of new skills, which pushes you to higher levels of performance. Second, they have clear goals and a system for feedback, so you know whether you are succeeding.

Aaron Kennedy and other leaders who have found the highest levels of success in the private sector are in search of their next optimal experience, the next opportunity to achieve flow.

A leadership job in government? That provides new and

varied challenges. It requires leaders to use their talents and learn new skills.

Challenge and Learning

Kristin Russell was considering another chief information officer (CIO) job with a major Fortune 500 company. The total compensation was more money than she had ever made in her entire career. But she didn't accept it.

Instead, she accepted a job for nearly one-sixth the salary working as secretary of technology and CIO for the state of Colorado. Of course, at first she was hesitant, as I described in the last chapter. She did not believe she had the right skill set. Initially, her husband did not want her to do it. And she was at the top of her earning potential as an executive in the tech industry, so the "cost" obstacle was on her mind.

When she made the final decision to do a stint in government, she did so for a number of reasons. But the most important, in Kristin's words, was that she was "ready for a change, a challenge. I had been in very senior executive leadership positions at great companies like Oracle. I was ready for a leadership adventure. To really put my leadership skills to the test in a way that might be useful."

Governor John Hickenlooper recognized this desire in Kristin. She met with him out of professional courtesy and curiosity when he was interviewing for his cabinet. At the time, she didn't intend to take the job.

At the start of their meeting, the governor and a few other cabinet members began asking her about the meaning of her life. What, to her, was the most important part of leading a great life? What was most important to her professionally? When she indicated that she just wanted to apply her leadership skills, to be useful, the governor hopped up from the table, went to his bookshelf, and pulled down a big book of poetry. He cleared his throat dramatically and said, "'To Be of Use.' It's a poem. May I read it to you?" Kristin was bewildered. She said yes for the first of two times that day. And after hearing the poem, something just clicked for Kristin. So she said yes again when the governor asked her if she would accept the job.

When the governor told me that he wooed Kristin Russell to take a leadership job in his cabinet with a poem, I must have wrinkled my nose in disbelief. "You read her a poem?" I asked. So he walked over to his bookshelf, opened the book, and with a straightforward and not too flowery tone recited the poem.

To Be of Use

The people I love the best
jump into work head first
without dallying in the shallows
and swim off with sure strokes almost out of sight.
They seem to become natives of that element,
the black sleek heads of seals
bouncing like half-submerged balls.

I love people who harness themselves, an ox to a heavy cart,
who pull like water buffalo, with massive patience,

who strain in the mud and the muck to move things forward,
who do what has to be done, again and again.

I want to be with people who submerge
in the task, who go into the fields to harvest
and work in a row and pass the bags along,

who are not parlor generals and field deserters
but move in a common rhythm
when the food must come in or the fire be put out.

The work of the world is common as mud.
Botched, it smears the hands, crumbles to dust.
But the thing worth doing well done
has a shape that satisfies, clean and evident.
Greek amphoras for wine or oil,
Hopi vases that held corn, are put in museums
but you know they were made to be used.
The pitcher cries for water to carry
and a person for work that is real.

—*Marge Piercy*

I got chills. *That is a powerful message,* I thought. *I bet that message resonates with a lot of successful private sector leaders— that they have more to give, and are searching for a way to give it.*

"I can see how that poem would speak to leaders who feel that they have so much more to contribute to the world," I told the governor. What I did not reveal was how it had struck a nerve with me as well, and in that moment, I decided quietly to do a stint in government myself at some point.

Kristin told me, "At that moment, he touched on a real need that I had—to do work that had meaning." Governor Hickenlooper was appealing to more than Kristin's sense of patriotic duty. He was not guilt-tripping her into accepting the job. He knew what you know—that people don't take jobs simply because others will benefit from their work. He knew that for Kristin to take this job, she would have to believe that there was something interesting and worthwhile in it for her. That she would have an opportunity to use and grow her leadership skills.

"I was getting a little bit bored, to be honest," said Kristin of her private sector career. "This government stint was going to be a new challenge, an exciting and somewhat mysterious new chapter in my career."

Did she regret it once she found herself in the new role? I caught up with Kristin after her first year in her new government job.

"Regrets? No regrets!" she said. "This has been as good an experience as I had hoped, maybe even a little bit better. The governor was not selling me a bill of goods."

She has had the most fun bringing best practices of leadership and management from the private sector into government. "I love that leadership ideas about organizational design, about strategy development and implementation, are really foreign concepts in the public sector," she added. "It's those things that I believe are the secret sauce of the private sector. The fact that I could make a difference was hugely valuable to me. And I could learn so much. I didn't know what they were talking about. I didn't know how government worked. But I've always been fascinated by those insurmountable challenges where I get to learn a ton. There's a quote from Vincent Van Gogh: 'I'm seeking. I'm striving. I'm in it with all my heart.' That is how I feel about this government chapter of my career."

Kristin's sense of stagnation with her previous job had surprised me, especially given her high-profile leadership career. But that was what Aaron Kennedy was saying, too. He told me that he has a high "need for challenge" score, according to the Birkman personality assessment he had taken. "People with high challenge scores take on big challenges for the satisfaction of tackling them, like 'Wow, that was a big thing and there aren't many people who could do that.' That's very satisfying to a high-challenge-score person. And it's hard to scratch that itch once you've already done it in the corporate world. Government would be a big new challenge. I don't know how many CEOs have high challenge scores, but I bet it's a lot."

Mark Emkes, CFO of the state of Tennessee, said his transition has been both a challenge and an education. Remember, Mark is the former CEO of Bridgestone Americas. He said to me, "Before I started, I didn't have a clue about state government or federal government. At Bridgestone, I started at the bottom and worked my way up to the top. Once I got to the top, I knew pretty much everything about the business. You come into state government in a high position and you're on a real steep learning curve. It has been extremely interesting, extremely educational. I'm working harder now than when I was as CEO!"

In *Flow*, Professor Csikszentmihalyi writes, "Contrary to what we usually believe . . . the best moments in our lives are not the passive, receptive, relaxing times—although such experiences can also be enjoyable, if we worked hard to attain them. The best moments usually occur when a person's body or mind is stretched to its limits in a voluntary effort to accomplish something difficult and worthwhile."[8]

Government leadership is exactly that: challenging and worthwhile. Governor Rick Snyder of Michigan said so: "It has been the best leadership adventure in terms of the most challenging and the most rewarding. It's been the experience of a lifetime."

It reminds me of being a parent. Is being a parent always

a pleasure cruise? No. A few weeks ago, my wife and I were attempting to have a quiet dinner with the kids. My son suddenly revealed the plastic baseball bat he was hiding under the table. He threw it across the table at my daughter and hit her in the mouth. Blood. Crying. Chaos ensued. But later that evening we got around to playing "Go Fish" and having some laughs over dessert. Do the daily challenges and difficulties mean it's not worth it to be a parent? No. It's totally worth it (for me, but I respect others who make a different choice). And maybe the challenges are part of what makes it so satisfying.

Governor Mitch Daniels may have said it best. I asked him if working in government is painful, worthwhile, or a great leadership adventure. He said, "Well, it is all of those things, sometimes all in the same day! But it is an enormous privilege." I asked him to rank his time as governor relative to his other leadership positions. He did not give me the answer I was hoping for, which is that it was the best. But he did say that his time as governor would rival his most satisfying leadership experience in the private sector, his time as president of North American operations with Eli Lilly.

Governor Jack Markell said that serving as governor, relative to his other jobs in his career, is "at the top in terms of challenge. It's hard for me to imagine that any other leadership experience could be more rewarding."

Just like marriage or having kids might become the best experience in your personal life, serving in government could become the best experience in your professional life.

Meaning and Worthwhile Goals

Governor Mitch Daniels has something special on his desk, something that allows him to see his state's progress relative to its goals. "I've got a dashboard on my desk with metrics from at least twenty-five key departments and agencies," he explained to me. "What people of talent have done in terms of improvement in the quality of public service here is enormously satisfying to me. And I know it's true because we measure everything."

That was interesting because it contradicts one of the obstacles of why great leaders avoid government. Many folks don't have confidence that they can make a difference in government. They are concerned that the bureaucracy will get in the way and make it impossible. Well, it's not impossible. Mitch Daniels's dashboard of success metrics gives him a profound sense of accomplishment. It suggests that a great private sector leader in government, using best practices of leadership, can make a difference and improve the quality of life for a society.

Governor Daniels reflected on why he got into government for the third time in his career. "When people said, 'Really, you're going to run for governor?' part of my answer would be, 'It's big enough to matter and it's executive office. There's a chance you could move some dirt. You could actually make things happen.'" And he has, on a massive scale. "My fellow citizens here or the papers may not notice all of the improvements. But I do, and the people who made it happen do. And I think that most of the folks who have joined us from the private sector feel good about what they did, and they can tell you why. I'm extraordinarily happy."

This story reminded me of a story Professor Csikszentmihalyi told of Rico. Rico was a factory worker who had been performing the same task more than six hundred times a day for five years and yet was still happy in his work. He achieved his happiness by setting daily goals to improve his speed. While he was sometimes rewarded with bonuses, he often wouldn't even tell others what he had achieved—"because when he is working at top performance the experience is so enthralling that it is almost painful for him to slow down."[9]

"When we choose a goal and invest ourselves in it to the limits of our concentration, whatever we do will be enjoyable," wrote Professor Csikszentmihalyi. "And once we have tasted this joy, we will redouble our efforts to taste it again. This is the way the self grows. Flow is important both because it makes the present instant more enjoyable, and because it builds the self-confidence that allows us to develop skills and make significant contributions to humankind."[10]

Fred Steingraber was leading a commission in Kenilworth, Illinois to examine how to achieve a sustainable budget. I described his work as an analyzer in leading a Blue Ribbon Commission in chapter 2.

Even before the commission was through with their work, people of the town were approaching Fred with the idea of his running for town president. Initially, and for a long time, he said no. Eventually, he changed his mind. I asked him what finally tipped the scales for him. "I said to myself, 'What the hell, I know where all the skeletons are. I know what the problems are. I even have a lot of ideas for how to deal with them.' And I thought about the consulting philosophy of Andrew Thomas Kearney, the firm I spent forty years with: you don't make recommendations that you are not prepared to implement yourself. So if I am making these recommendations, and I feel they're appropriate, I ought to be willing to spend the time to get them executed."

And that is exactly what he has done. But does he find

his work in government painful, worthwhile, or a fun leadership adventure?

"I'm having great fun. These ideas are working and I get a lot of gratification from it. People I don't know call me or write me notes thanking me for what I'm doing. I think there is a high level of trust and confidence in the town that we're doing sensible things, and the village is benefitting as a result."

Did he just say "fun?" The former CEO of a billion-dollar company, A.T. Kearney, says that his time in government has been *fun*. It's fun to use your leadership skills. It's fun to take on big challenges. It is fun to have people send you letters of thanks. It makes you feel good, to be of use.

Sure, there are stresses in government leadership. Kristin told me about expressing frustration to her husband about the daunting challenges she was facing as state CIO. "I was talking to my husband, saying, 'Oh my gosh, I'm so stressed.' And he said, 'Kristin, do you think you're going to fix government? Because you're not going to fix government.' I know I'm not going to fix government entirely, but I want it to suck less. I know not everything will be hit-the-ball-out-of-the-park great. And that's okay. Because what we are doing is making government work better than it was working, and I'm proud of the progress."

Variety of Relationships

There is one more "what's in it for you" to serving in government: the variety of people you get to meet and work with.

Governor Hickenlooper told me, "In business, leaders tend to interact with a lot of the same types of people. But in this job, you get to interact with an amazing range of people— to build relationships with them, to help them in ways that only you can. It's really pretty amazing to have this feeling of being a part of a broader community, and to play a role in making people's lives better."

For Earl Goode, the former senior executive of GTE who is today chief of staff to Governor Mitch Daniels, the variety of relationships he has enjoyed has been a satisfying aspect of his work in government. "Every day you get a call or an email from somebody who has a problem. I'd say for eight out of ten people who need something, we're able to help. You can really help."

• • •

A generation ago, what people cared most about at work was making money. Increasingly, what people care about today is making a difference.

So as you consider doing a stint in government, please don't avoid it because you fear it is only going to bring you pain. It is not.

Don't avoid it because you think it might be a worthwhile patriotic duty that benefits others but not you. And don't consider it just because you think you "ought" to, or because you feel you owe society something beyond the value you contributed in the private sector.

You don't owe anybody anything. You have contributed value in building valuable companies, in bringing innovative and high quality products and services to market. You have provided people with jobs. And you have paid far more in taxes than the value of services you receive from our government.

Do a stint in government because there is a good chance that it will become your most satisfying leadership experience of your career. You will get

- Challenge and learning
- Meaning and worthwhile goals
- Variety of relationships

That is what's in it for you.

And what's in it for us, the citizens, is that we get a higher-performing government that improves everyone's quality of life.

How can we make leadocracy happen? The next challenge is to improve how we do our job as voters, to be able to choose the best leaders out of the slate of candidates, to vote smart.

The Leadocracy Discussion

1. When have you experienced flow at work?
2. What would be the strongest reason for you to consider a stint in government leadership—using your skills, learning new ones, being challenged, creating meaning, or building relationships?
3. Can you imagine any other benefits of serving in government?

CHAPTER 6

Vote Smart

The led must not be compelled;
they must be able to choose their own leader.
—Albert Einstein

Democracy works best when voters choose great candidates.

The problem is, we're not so good at doing that. And we feel burned. The sign of a broken hiring process is being constantly surprised by the bad result: "That person did not turn out to be what I thought they were!" means that it is time to improve the process.

In this chapter, let's think together about why we make mistakes as voters. I'll suggest a simple checklist that might help us do a better job as voters. And let's start to think about the types of candidates we should avoid putting into office.

"Only people who have an incredibly strong need for the power of a political position and a limited self-awareness of their own shortcomings seem to thrive in the world of government," Aaron Kennedy said to me.

"Unfortunately, I think we are getting more and more of those kinds of people in government today," he concluded.

Today, voters select government leaders based on things

that do not have anything to do with how well the person will perform in the job. And we often get it wrong as a result.

This behavior is not limited to selecting political leaders. I've seen poor leadership selection in all types of organizations. I was once helping the board of a Fortune 500 company select a new CEO. I had interviewed every member of the board about priorities and desired results and designed a CEO scorecard. Based on that scorecard and many interviews, I identified the candidate who was a very good match with what that situation required. This was after spending over five hours interviewing this candidate. His leadership results were impressive. The relevance of his talents to this particular situation was amazing. He exhibited all three great leadership behaviors—analyzing, allocating, and aligning—in spades.

But do you know what the board said? They said no, they didn't want to hire him *because he dressed poorly*. One board member asked, "How would he look on TV? How believable will he be to the analyst community? Besides, you know, he doesn't *look* like a CEO." There was some talk of his haircut. I felt frustration building. Searing outrage spread through my body. This guy was a great leader, and the board wasn't going to hire him because he didn't *look* like a CEO? *This is insanity*, I thought.

The end of the story is a positive one. I controlled my frustration and reviewed the scorecard with the board, the scorecard which they had created for this role. We rated each candidate on all of the outcomes and competencies. They concluded that this candidate's leadership achievement record did in fact *crush* every important criterion. It's like they snapped out of their temporary insanity, stopped thinking about the

Today, voters select government leaders based on things that do not have anything to do with how well the person will perform in the job. And we often get it wrong as a result.

candidate's haircut for a minute, and realized that he was a great match. They hired him. And this new CEO *crushed* their performance targets and delivered them a big win.

I wondered how often this same pitfall influences how we vote to hire government leaders. And I think *hire* is the right word. Whether we are voting or appointing or hiring in the more traditional sense, we are selecting somebody to do a job for us, with specific responsibilities and paying them to do that job. Government is no exception. We, the citizens, are paying their salary. We are hiring them. So let's choose wisely.

Voodoo Voting

In our book on hiring, *Who*, Randy Street and I talk about "voodoo hiring" methods. Voodoo hiring involves too much use of gut feel, a lack of structured interviews, a complete absence of process, etc. In elections, we often make the same mistakes.

As voters, we don't hire well. We vote for the guy or gal with the nice suit and the great hair. Or as studies have shown, the person on the ballot whose name sounds most familiar. We fall in love with candidates who can give a great speech. We use appearance as a proxy for leadership competence. What rarely happens is a serious, analytical assessment of a candidate's actual leadership capability relative to the task at hand.

I once observed a candidate running for office who kept emphasizing how average he was. He seemed to take pride in telling the audience about his failures in business. He explained that he hadn't achieved great things, that he had suffered through difficult times, just like his fellow voters.

I'm a student of psychology, so of course I knew what he was doing. It's an age-old form of manipulation. "Vote for me. I'm just a regular guy like you. I'm likable. I feel your pain. I can identify with you and you can identify with me."

I kept thinking, *What a crazy message this is*. Not to mention insulting to his audience. Does a city appoint most average citizens to play on its professional basketball team? Of course not. That would be silly. Imagine an announcer's voice over the loudspeaker: "For the home team, number 13, standing at five feet seven inches and two hundred pounds, a shooting guard who played JV basketball in high school during a semester ten years ago . . . John Smiiiiithh!"

Ridiculous, right?

Not to voters, apparently. The bizarre thing is, that candidate with the "I'm just an average Joe" message won the election! And then he proceeded to turn in the average performance we should have expected, wasting taxpayer money and adding layers to the bureaucracy.

I like the idea of every citizen of a certain age voting. But I don't like the idea of electing people of average leadership ability. I'd rather we elect our superstars, the most talented and skillful leaders in our society, leaders who will deliver much better results than the average citizen might. When we get those great leaders in office, we get a better return on that leader's salary. A better return on tax investment. A better return on government spending.

I had to discover why we were going with "average Joe." I watched the pundits talk about candidates, reviewed research on voting influences, watched speeches. What I learned is that we default to a handful of "voodoo voting" methods that leave us perpetually disappointed in our elected officials.

Voodoo Voting

- We place too much emphasis on likability.
- We place too much emphasis on public-speaking ability and debates.
- We place too much emphasis on a single hot-button issue that has little to do with our overall quality of life and the real problems that plague our communities.
- We place too much emphasis on the physical attractiveness of the candidates.
- We tend to be lulled into following candidates who "feel our pain" and merely *reflect* their understanding of our problems, but who do not have the demonstrated ability to *solve* them.

Debates are not a very valid predictor of job performance, by the way. They rely on several mechanisms that don't work in predicting job performance. In graduate school, I read literally thousands of studies on the topic of leadership selection, conducted over the last half-century. One thing I learned is that the act of asking people *hypothetical* questions—like the ones asked during debates—does not give you an accurate prediction of how they will perform in a job. What people say they "would do" rarely turns out to be true. Hypothetical questions give candidates too much opportunity to "snow" the evaluator with a clever answer. In contrast, a better predictor of success is what a candidate has *achieved* in their career. Questions that get at what a candidate has actually accomplished, and how, are much better predictors of job performance.

Voodoo voting creates a self-defeating cycle: (1) Good-looking candidate gives good speeches reflecting their understanding of our pain. (2) We trust them to solve our problems.

(3) They don't solve our problems and we feel increasingly frustrated and betrayed, and so (4) we pin our hopes on the next candidate who comes along looking good and giving good speeches and reflecting their understanding of our pain . . . and the cycle repeats.

And the damned debate format exacerbates this "he who has the best hair and the zingy-est one-liners wins" sort of theater. Watch videos of the superstar governors I have been talking about in this book: Mitch Daniels, Jack Markell, Rick Snyder, and John Hickenlooper. You will notice something peculiar. They are not the best public speakers you have ever seen. Some of them even joke about being dry, unpolished, or "no frills" in their public speaking style. They are direct. They are known for what they accomplish in the job, not just known for how they give a speech.

Voodoo voting happens when voters select the wrong candidates. Voodoo hiring also happens when those wrong candidates hire the wrong managers under them. Voodoo hiring happens at many levels of government, from top-level appointments to front-line supervisors, which results in cascading mediocrity and sub-par performances. So how can we change our habits as voters to hire better leaders into office?

A Better Way to Hire

Ken Griffin is the founder and CEO of Citadel, one of the most successful investment firms in the world because of the talent it attracts. This is one of those "I started my business out of a Harvard dorm room" self-made multibillionaire types whom we read about in *Forbes*. To give you a sense of how smart Ken is, consider this fact: some of the smartest people I have ever met have told me that Ken is the smartest person they have ever met. So let's see what he thinks we can do to improve our voting skill.

Ken has an idea of how we can break the cycle of voo-doo voting. "As a nation, we need to get really focused on track records and less focused on who gives the great speech. We need to focus on the question, 'Does this person have the relevant experiences from which I can determine whether he or she will be successful as a leader?' A set of accomplishments and failures gives us a richness of information upon which to make decisions. That's how we need to think about candidates."

Governor Jack Markell has an eye for leadership talent. When I asked him about his method for hiring leaders, he said, "The head of my economic development office was probably the most respected business leader in Delaware. He built a chain of seventy-six drug stores and sold it to Walgreens. He knows business inside and out. He had proven his leadership skill in the private sector. I have other people who have been in government for a long time and have political savvy. I've got a tremendous team, some of whom I've known for years, some of whom I did not meet until I interviewed them. I took a couple people from out of state because I think having the infusion of new ideas can always be valuable. I have a range in ages from twenty-nine to mid-sixties." From this description, I could tell that what matters most to Governor Markell is leadership experience, results, and relevance.

But leadership competence can be missed if you aren't specifically looking for it. And that is where practical tools can be valuable.

"I'm a huge believer that talent management in the government sector is not done as well as it could be," Mark Gal-logly said to me. I first told you about Mark and his impressive leadership background in chapter 1 (he is the cofounder of Centerbridge Partners, who advised me to take up Ben Franklin's practice of meeting regularly with talented people from the community). "What you have to try to do is identify a scorecard for these roles."

Based on the vast literature on candidate selection, on my firm's nearly twenty years in business, and the research Randy Street and I did for *Who: The A Method for Hiring*, I've adapted two tools that voters and elected government leaders might find valuable.

In *Who*, we introduce the "A Method for Hiring," which includes four steps: (1) scorecard, (2) source, (3) select, and (4) sell. Since sourcing political candidates and selling them on taking the job is outside of the realm of a voter, we'll not focus on those two steps here. The two steps we will focus on are scorecard (how to articulate the success criteria) and select (how to collect and analyze data to make a great decision).

I believe these tools could help create a shift in mind-set for us all.

The Leadocracy Scorecard

The first tool I have prepared for you is the Leadocracy Scorecard.

The essence of a scorecard is two-fold:

1. To identify the list of measurable outcomes that you want the candidate to achieve. It could be balancing a budget (of $10 billion, for example), improving performance in a specific area (reducing homelessness by 30 percent), or taking steps toward solving a broader economic or community problem (reducing unemployment from 9 percent to 6 percent by a certain date).

2. To identify the list of competencies that you think are relevant and important for the job. A checklist of competencies is provided on the next page. Just "star" the ones you think might be particularly important for the job.

Then you go collect data on each candidate. Collecting data is pretty easy these days—read their bios on Wikipedia; read their books (most of the candidates for big offices have a book); listen to long biographical interviews on shows like *Charlie Rose* where you can hear what they accomplished and how they accomplished it; and read news stories about what they achieved and how.

Then you rate each candidate, based on the facts and data you collected, not on gut feeling or hairstyles or how well they tell jokes on *The Tonight Show*.

Now tally your scores. You will vote for the candidate with the highest overall score.

While this chapter is mostly focused on voting, this simple hiring process works for elected officials appointing their key hires as well. Heck, this process works for hiring a gardener, a babysitter, a company to clean out the leaves from your gutter, an executive assistant, a wedding planner, a CEO, a call center worker, a not-for-profit fundraiser, or a nanotechnology researcher.

This approach works to hire anybody for anything.

It certainly can work for hiring leaders for elective or appointed office.

There is a lot of information out there on candidates, and you may find that much of it is conflicting. To interpret the data that you gather and assign accurate scores on the Leadocracy Scorecard, ask yourself these two important questions about the outcomes the leader has achieved:

The Leadocracy Scorecard

Candidate Name: _____

Outcomes I Expect Leader to Achieve	Rating: 1 (low) – 10 (high) Based on the results this leader has achieved and their relevance to these outcomes

COMPETENCIES	Rating: 1 (low) – 10 (high) Based on the results this leader has achieved and their relevance to these competencies
ANALYZING	
Learns quickly	
Thinks critically and strategically	
Is creative and innovative	
Is attentive to detail	
Listens effectively	
Invites criticism and sharing of ideas	
ALLOCATING	
Focuses on planning and efficient systems and organization	
Hires A players, develops people, and removes underperformers	
Seeks the best value from resources	
Prioritizes based on needs, not wants	
Is customer and service focused	
Sets high standards and holds people accountable	
ALIGNING	
Treats others with respect, but stands up for beliefs	
Is flexible and adaptable, yet persistent	
Focuses on efficient execution	
Motivates others through enthusiasm and pragmatic optimism	
Demonstrates integrity, honesty, and work ethic	
Follows through on commitments	
Is a persuasive communicator	

Note: Adapted from ghSMART & Co. and used with permission.

Results: To what extent has this candidate achieved great *results* as a leader?

Relevance: How *relevant* are the candidate's past results to the outcomes you desire?

For instance, if one of the outcomes you want is a balanced budget of a certain size ask, *Has this candidate successfully balanced budgets in his or her career of about that size? Was that experience relevant to the budget issues we face?*

Let's say that one candidate seems to have performed very well in turning around two unprofitable companies, moving them from huge losses to solid financial footing. She also balanced a large budget while working with a not-for-profit organization that had been operating with a deficit and accumulating debt. You might rate the candidate as a 9 or 10 for that outcome, right? If the candidate had experience leading an organization with a big budget, but the budget was sound when he took over and sound when he left, you might rate her as a 5. And if the candidate has not had any apparent experience leading an organization or department with a large budget, or has tried and failed to do so, you might rate her a 1 or 2 on that outcome area.

For the competency section, ask yourself the same two questions for each of the 3 As. Reflect on all the information you have about what the candidate has actually done, and rate their performance in those competency areas. The following questions can help you:

Analyzing

Results: To what extent has this candidate delivered impressive results as an analyzer?

Relevance: How relevant are this candidate's analyzing achievements to the tasks at hand?

Allocating

Results: To what extent has this candidate delivered impressive results as an allocator?

Relevance: To what extent are this candidate's allocating achievements relevant to the tasks at hand?

Aligning

Results: To what extent has this candidate delivered impressive results as an aligner?

Relevance: To what extent are this candidate's aligning achievements relevant to the tasks at hand?

If I could summarize everything I know about hiring candidates into one piece of advice, if would be this: vote for candidates who have achieved the magnitude and relevance of results that fit the situation.

Let's look at some examples of how this test might be used. Assume that we're trying to elect a leader to handle a tough job with three top priorities: balancing a fairly large budget, creating more jobs in the community, and expanding certain services with fewer resources.

Consider candidate A: He is a career lawyer of modest academic performance who has never led a team of more than four people, and who has been involved in politics for many years. People who have worked with him are saying in the media that he is divisive, a naysayer who performed poorly relative to his peer group in his jobs. He has served on a few commissions, but those commissions never accomplished anything noteworthy. He does not seem to have much demonstrated talent in any of the 3 As, has no real results to show, and has no particularly relevant skill sets. He would rate poorly for the outcomes and the competencies.

Now consider candidate B: She was the CEO of an entrepreneurial company, growing it from $50 million to $250 million in revenue over seven years, and from three hundred jobs to over 1,500 jobs. She consistently led the company to beat profit goals while turning out some of the most innovative products in the industry. The company has amazing customer loyalty. She was previously a senior leader at one of the most admired companies in the world, where she was responsible for turning around a struggling division. This candidate's leadership track record rates high in magnitude of results and relevance. You can feel confident that she would bring a high level of leadership talent and a focus on results that would allow her to achieve many more good things with the same or fewer resources.

I know this approach to hiring can work in government because we have been applying it with great success in the state of Colorado. Governor Hickenlooper has used this approach in many contexts—selecting senior cabinet hires, training all of his department heads, setting out his own goals for his first term, and even nominating a Supreme Court justice. We have received kudos and thanks from government leaders who are using this method successfully in areas as varied as economic development, human services, healthcare, legal, personnel administration, and labor relations.

Leader Achievement Record

The second best practice of hiring we'll adapt to the context of voting is the "select" step of the method laid out in *Who*. This is the step where you collect data on candidates, analyze it, and make your decision on who to vote for.

We live in a world that is based on the sound bite. Sound bites are nice. But it would be easier to select great leaders if we knew more about *what they had really achieved* in their careers. I would urge every candidate for elective office to complete a "Leader Achievement Record" to help voters separate facts from rhetoric.

I find that many candidates conjure up a smokescreen to keep the voter from the truth—their less than impressive experience and results. They try to distract voters the way a parent might try to distract an upset child: "No, you can't have a piece of candy . . . Hey, look at those pretty birds!" Or "No, I don't really have any solid experience . . . Hey, did you know the other candidate groped his secretary?"

Great, talented leaders do the opposite. They clearly articulate the facts of their achievements, because they have leadership achievements to articulate!

One simple format might look like what we in the field call a biographical interview. This type of interview traces its roots to an in-depth interviewing approach pioneered by my father, Brad Smart, nearly half a century ago. At ghSMART, we have continued to innovate on this approach over the past two decades. My dad calls his current version of this style of interviewing a Topgrading Interview. The ghSMART version of this interview is called the "Who Interview," as in "this interview reveals *who* someone really is."

Here, I'm going to call it the Leader Achievement Record. It should be a matter of public record for every candidate seeking a public office. Here is how it works, very simply. Candidates could complete the Leaders Achievement Record and post it on their websites. Or they could subject themselves to an in-depth interview that would be posted, unedited, on their websites. That would be extremely helpful to understand the person for who they really are.

The Leader Achievement Record

1. What were your most impressive leadership achievements during your school years?

2. For every job you have had, please provide the following information:
   - Name of employer, dates of employment, title, name of boss
   - What were you hired to achieve?
   - What leadership achievements were you most proud of?
   - What were your greatest mistakes you made as a leader in that job?
   - What will your boss and coworkers say were your greatest leadership strengths and weaknesses?
   - Why did you leave that job?

That's it! These are such simple questions, but can you imagine how clearly we would understand a candidate with this information? Imagine how well informed our decisions would be. This approach could really help voters separate the wheat from the chaff, the big doers from the big talkers, the leaders of substance from the spin-masters.

Red Flags

You may be wondering, "Are there any specific types of candidates we as voters should avoid?" The short answer is no. I don't like stereotyping. What matters most is doing just a little bit of homework—writing your Leadocracy Scorecard for the role, then collecting data on a candidate and building a Leader Achievement Record.

However, if you insist on knowing the set of red flags I

personally look out for when evaluating candidates, here they are. I am not angry at these types of candidates for trying to get elected; I don't think they are all bad people. Many have perfectly honorable intentions. It's just that these profiles often signal an absence of real leadership ability.

The Bureaucrat

Spot the bureaucrat by listening to what they say is "wrong."

Often, their diagnosis of what is "wrong" involves government having insufficient rules, regulations, laws, burdens, oversight, and constraints. They suggest solutions that impose more burdens and restrictions on citizens. They show how "experienced" they are by listing out all the committees, regulatory agencies, and councils they have sat on—groups that likely made recommendations, suggestions, or declarations but achieved not much of measurable value. There is also sort of a demonizing behavior you see with bureaucrats, where they point the finger at some criminal, for example, and then overreact in the new restrictions they want to place over citizens, to prevent more of that behavior. Watch out for career politicians, especially those who have only served in the legislative branch their entire lives, those who are very chummy with special-interest groups, and those who always seem to be jockeying for power rather than solving problems.

Now, there are career politicians who are not bureaucratic and who are great leaders. But I haven't seen many!

The Turtle

The turtle isn't a candidate who is slow. Instead, "turtle" refers to the saying: "If you find a turtle on top of a fence post, someone put him there." Obviously, turtles can't climb up a fence post—I guess they lack the claws or strength or joints or courage. It takes someone else's effort to put a turtle on a fence post.

In other words, sometimes people get to great heights not based on their talents. Instead, they were put there by privilege (which is driven by someone else's talent) or by being in the right place at the right time.

If you want to spot a turtle, look for poor grades at elite universities. Be suspicious of name-dropping and people who have been *around* greatness, but who have not contributed to it.

Watch for lackluster results. And listen for people who don't give much credit to the people who have helped them get where they are (because they are trying to hide them behind the curtain).

Now, there are people of privilege who have developed strong leadership skills. Just because you were born into a wealthy family does not make you a bad candidate for government. However, just make sure when you are considering whom to vote for that you are not mistaking someone's opportunities for the real results they have achieved.

Let's not mistake "pedigree" for "performance."

The Screamer

Voters must think these screamers have passion and the courage to "fight for me" or to "take on the other group." It's the easiest way to work a crowd of supporters into a cheering frenzy.

But screamers are often just blowhards. They blame and point fingers. They manufacture controversy. They whine and complain. But they don't achieve much of note. Voters often regret their decision to vote for screamers. George Washington was not a screamer. Abraham Lincoln was not a screamer.

John F. Kennedy was not a screamer. Ronald Reagan was not a screamer. I REST MY CASE, DAMMIT! (Just kidding.)

Now, just because a candidate screams, that does not automatically mean he is unqualified. But if you find that his primary tactic for getting elected is screaming the loudest or "out-passioning" the other candidates, beware.

Let's not mistake "passion" for "performance."

The Idealist

The idealist is a candidate who promises much but delivers little. Watch for excessive use of the words *ought* and *need*. "We ought to give a break to hardworking Americans." "We need to improve benefits for the elderly." "There ought to be a cure for malaria."

Here is another entertaining "Jedi mind trick" that Idealists use as a rhetorical sleight of hand: "My opponent has tried for years, every chance he gets, to tear up the Constitution/promote child abuse/rob the elderly/enslave working class people." Or this one: "My opponent hates America." *Really? Your opponent has been trying to tear up the Constitution? To promote child abuse? To rob the elderly? To literally enslave working class people? How awful. And your opponent hates the country?* This ideological rhetoric is what poor leaders use to try to brainwash voters into siding with them.

The impractical idealist rarely talks about trade-offs or substantive plans. They rarely talk about how to pay for the programs that we "ought" to introduce for the people who "need" them. Pay particular attention to the cake-and-eat-it-too logic of the impractical ideologue, as in "We need to make the environment cleaner without putting any burdens on businesses." Huh? Wait, what? What exactly are you suggesting?

In the private sector, that kind of idealist non-logic would be as silly as saying something like, "As CEO, I have decided that we have to move our headquarters to another state. But don't worry, our intent is not to disrupt any of our employees' families." Well, dude, moving people thousands of miles away from their kids' schools, friends, and extended family members is disruptive. Decisions have consequences. Idealists seem to suggest that if you follow their ideals, everything will be peachy. But when you try to follow the logic of what they are proposing, you often find that either the math does not add up or the language they use is not meant to solve problems but instead is there to polarize voters.

Of course, not all people who feel strongly about their ideology are bad candidates. There are some folks whose ideology is in fact quite practical and useful for society. However, let's make sure there is more to a candidate's leadership skill than the ability to polarize a group based on ideology.

Let's not mistake "ideology" for "problem solving."

• • •

I hope you will considering using the Leadocracy Scorecard and the Leader Achievement Record to vote smarter. Now that we have covered the "scorecard" and "select" steps that are used any good hiring process, let's take a crack at the "source" step (how to get more great leaders interested in government) in the next chapter.

The Leadocracy Discussion

1. Admit it, how much has a candidate's appearance swayed your opinion of him or her in previous elections?
2. What other voodoo voting habits do you see? How do they lead to the wrong candidates being elected?
3. What other new, innovative methods could we as voters use get better data and facts about our candidates' career performance? What could prevent us from over-relying on debates and news media sound bites?

CHAPTER 7

The Leaders Initiative

*Effective leadership is putting first things first. Effective
management is discipline, carrying it out.*
—*Stephen Covey*

I want to live in a leadocracy.

With more great leaders serving in the public sector, the
performance of government will go up, burdens and bureaucratic waste will go down, and the quality of life for everyone
will go up.

There are three things I am doing to try to advance the
cause. First, I volunteer my time to advise government leaders on how to implement the principles in this book. Second,
I wrote this book to try to get the word out. Third, I founded
The Leaders Initiative (TLI). This not-for-profit organization's mission is "to elevate humanity by identifying, developing, and deploying society's greatest leaders into government."

So I'm not just sitting here behind my desk saying what
you "ought" to do. I'm trying to lead by example and experiment with a concept to go get great leaders and bring them
into government. The Leaders Initiative is not the only

solution. It is not the best solution. Other people will come up with even better ideas. It's just *an* idea to make it easier and less painful for great leaders to dip a toe into government—to prime the pump.

Not many private sector leaders want to even consider a job in government.

As I mentioned in the introduction, University of Chicago entrepreneurship professor Steve Kaplan and his research team found that only 2 percent of CEOs expressed any interest in serving in government (out of a sample of 307 CEOs).

It would be better for all of us if that number were closer to 80 percent. It would be a dream come true if the banter you heard among CEOs was "Did you sign the Leadocracy Pledge? Me too. I'm not going to do my two-year leadership service term for probably five years, but I'm starting now to learn more about my government to figure out where I might be of use."

Why two years? Because it is long enough to be meaningful, and short enough to not be too disruptive in someone's career. It worked for Wendy Kopp.

Teach For America founder Wendy Kopp had a vision of providing a high-quality education to all students in the country, regardless of their location or background. When I called Wendy to discuss how she built Teach For America, I was impressed by her drive and generosity of spirit. Her approach was to select the very best and brightest university graduates and send them into low-income communities to teach for two years. These teachers would have a chance to do something meaningful and challenging. The priorities, career paths, and decisions of a generation of future leaders would be affected. Many chose to stay in the education-reform movement, like

KIPP founders Mike Feinberg and Dave Levin (cofounders of the largest charter-school operator in the country). And the students in those low-income communities received the benefit of smart, energetic teachers.

Why don't we do that for government? Imagine an organization that identifies society's greatest leaders not currently serving in government, helps those leaders learn about government service and develop an understanding of how to be successful, and then deploys them into a two-year leadership service stint in a government leadership role.

Maybe some leaders would return to their nongovernment lives after their term is up and hand the baton to the next great leader. Or some might choose to stay in government for a longer term. Some might even run for an elected office. This was the idea we developed in Governor Hickenlooper's office many months ago, when he was faced with the daunting challenge of hiring his cabinet.

A few months after that meeting, I founded The Leaders Initiative (501(c)(3) status pending).

Through that organization, we are working to advance the concept of leadocracy very directly. We are, as my mom says, "taking them by the scruff of the neck" and pulling, I mean gently coaxing, them into government.

As Roxane White, Governor Hickenlooper's chief of staff, described, this plan is reminiscent of the type of civic involvement we had around the time of the founding of this country. The best leaders would step forward and apply their talents for the good of their communities. Ben Franklin is just one example. He was a businessperson, an entrepreneur, and an amazing inventor. He became involved in government and achieved spectacular leadership feats, editing the Declaration of Independence, signing the U.S. Constitution, and serving as president of Pennsylvania, ambassador to France, and the first U.S. postmaster general. He was focused on applying his leadership talents for the good of everyone. And he seemed to have fun with it.

When Roxane raised that point, it reminded me of my friend Mark's suggestion to start a civic group years earlier. And Professor Csikszentmihalyi made a similar observation—that the ancient Romans (when their civilization was strong, long before it crumbled) used to have similar community meetings. There would be some social problem, perhaps the water supply. Then some merchant would raise his hands and say, "OK, I'll work on that." People would have a quick vote, and off he went. It is a very natural thing for citizens to run their own governments. I think it is a less natural phenomenon to expect people to go into government their entire lives without the benefit of ever really living in the society they are supposed to be governing.

This model resonates with me on a deep level. I'm a direct descendent of Governor William Bradford of Plymouth Colony, who sailed on the Mayflower to the New World and became one of our country's first governors. He worked as a weaver in a shop he owned before he got into government at age thirty-one. Governor Bradford is credited with creating the enduring American traditions of Thanksgiving, private ownership of property, freedom of speech via town hall meetings, and a free press. He was reelected governor an astonishing thirty times. (This brings up the problem of term limits, but the point I was making is that he was a great leader who made a great impact by moving from the private sector to government).

Many leaders seem to think there is this big iron curtain

standing between the private sector and the government sector. There isn't. There is no brick or barbed wire. The iron curtain of ignorance is really just a window drapery—thin and flimsy and easy to move aside. The challenge becomes how to pull aside this drapery, demystify government to these great leaders, and give them a path to service.

The Leader's Career Arc

Mark Gallogly, managing principal of investment firm Centerbridge Partners and member of President Obama's Council on Jobs and Competitiveness, summarized the problem we face in hiring government leaders. "The United States has historically had no clear policy to attract great talent into government on a consistent and rigorous basis. Every administration comes in with five thousand appointments to fill at the federal level. How can we consistently fill these appointments with a broad range of talented executives?"

There are vast numbers of appointed leadership positions not only at the federal level but also at the state and local levels. These appointed leaders are often the people responsible for leading a business unit of the government (also known as a department) to achieve results. To say it's where the "real work" happens is not fully respectful to the other branches. But let's just say the people who actually deliver you most of the services you receive from government are not spending their time bickering in Congress—they are out analyzing problems, allocating billions of dollars and thousands of employees, and aligning to get stuff done. These people are appointed cabinet members and their staffs.

I understand that it takes a lot to *run* for elected office. Most of the fears I heard from leaders about government service are amplified when you start talking about campaigning and polls. Trying to convince masses of leaders to run for elected office seemed like a losing battle to me.

So that is why with TLI, we are choosing to start with appointed roles in the state government. No campaigns. No big scrutiny from the press.

Sound more doable?

Of the great leaders I spoke with who actually took the plunge into government, many never considered public service until they were asked to serve. Most private sector leaders work hard in school, they build their careers, and then they get out of the grind and start serving on boards, maybe start a few foundations, and finally retire to the golf course. It is the typical career arc of a leader: make good grades, make a buck, make a difference, make a putt. And in all that make-a-difference time, they do not consider having a chapter of public service. And many, many leaders feel "empty," "bored," "unengaged," and "hollow" by the time they give up the corner office. Here is a hint: don't retire just yet. Instead, do a stint in government and stay active.

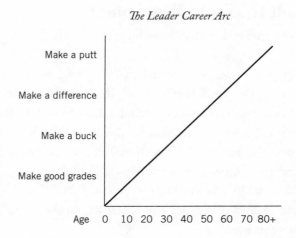

The Leader Career Arc

That "make a difference" stage is an important one. New York City mayor Michael Bloomberg once said, "What I've done is I've attracted some very great people to government. People who could make a lot more money in the private sector, but have chosen government. Sometimes I was the first one to even suggest to them that it would be a great place, because they can change the world. And they have changed the world."[11]

We have a poor system for attracting talent into the public sector, and we do little to help great leaders understand the leadership opportunity it presents. We are not recognizing their willingness to contribute during the "make a difference" stage of their lives. It is a rare leader, like Governor Rick Snyder, who plans to serve in government at some point in his or her career. Governor Snyder developed his plan when he was still in college to serve at some point between the ages of forty and sixty. But there are few people with that kind of foresight.

This is the problem I hope The Leaders Initiative will solve.

If We Built It, Would They Come?

But would our greatest leaders be willing to join The Leaders Initiative?

Figuring out whom we wanted in this group was easy. Governor Hickenlooper, Chief of Staff Roxane White, and I compared notes on the publicly available lists of Colorado's "most powerful leaders" assembled by the local newspapers. We examined the roster of professional organizations like Young Presidents' Organization and World Presidents' Organization. We consulted lists of highest-paid CEOs. We talked with our friends and colleagues and asked whom they would nominate for this group.

As of the writing of this book, of the first seven leaders we asked to join this group, all seven said they are "in"!

Aaron Kennedy, the founder of Noodles & Company, is "in." When I asked him about being part of The Leaders Initiative, he said, "I don't really know how to access the training and develop the skills to succeed in government. Would this help me become successful in influencing government, either inside of it or out of it? Would being involved in this organization assist me in stepping in and making a contribution in government successfully? What is the caliber of the people involved in the organization? Would I learn a lot? Would it be stimulating? Would it be a rewarding use of my time? I might be interested if you made me feel that this would be a great way to make a philanthropic impact in the world or my community and it would be a better use of my time and money." I answered these questions for Aaron (you will learn more about how TLI operates in a moment).

Mike Fries is "in." Mike is the CEO of an international cable TV company he helped build called Liberty Global. Today Liberty Global has a whopping $10 billion in revenue with over twenty thousand employees. And Mike has an artistic side—he sings lead vocals in a rock band. He is a fun guy, not just a "suit."

Christine Kneeland is "in." Christine is an entrepreneur who specializes in organizational and leadership development and is COO of Center Partners. She came highly recommended by the private sector and government leaders we consulted.

Jandel Allen-Davis is "in." She was a medical doctor who rose to be a senior leader in the giant Kaiser Permanente health services company in Colorado.

Mary Pat Link is "in." She is founder of an Inc. 500 (the 500 fastest growing firms in the United States) company called Interlink, and was awarded the prestigious Ernst & Young Entrepreneur of the Year award for Colorado.

Dave Hoover is "in!" He is chairman of Ball Corporation, which has $8 billion in revenue. Bloomberg once called Dave the #2 best CEO in the United States based on his leadership and financial results.

Kent Thiry said he is "in." Kent is CEO of DaVita, a $7 billion company with 40,000 employees that was on *Fortune*'s 2009 list of "Top Companies for Leaders." Stanford Business School and Harvard Business School each wrote a case study on Kent's leadership.

Wow! WOW! WOW! These are the greatest leaders we identified from our entire state. And they all said yes. Maybe there is hope for leadocracy after all.

"I've never seen so many members of the business community so passionately involved in politics as I have in recent months," Ken Griffin, CEO of the vastly successful investment company Citadel, told me. It was a trend I was happy to hear about. When I asked Ken if he would consider becoming more involved, he said, "I would have to consider becoming formally involved if a future president of the United States asked me to serve on behalf of our nation. It's time we move beyond the empty rhetoric that fills the halls of Washington. Working with someone like Mitch Daniels or Paul Ryan, leaders who embrace the kind of changes needed to secure our country's future, would be great privilege. I want to leave my children and grandchildren an America that is once again a land of opportunity, a place where they too can pursue their dreams. Returning America to a land of opportunity is the legacy my generation needs to leave behind."

Like the leaders I spoke with who did make the leap, Ken is interested in working with talented leaders. That is why Kristin Russell made the leap. That is why Mark Emkes made the leap. That is why Earl Goode made the leap. They were attracted to governors who were focused on results, not on rhetoric.

If we want better leadership in government, we have to convince our best leaders that it is worth it to them to serve. And we have to help break down as many obstacles as possible. Because a government is only as good as those who serve in it.

The Idea and the Plan

We have not yet figured out how the entire Leaders Initiative program will ultimately be designed. Our founding group is assembled, but we have not met yet to strategize. And I will soon customize the design of the program to fit leaders' needs and preferences. However, we have established some core principles and our first steps.

First, we are in the process of identifying the fifteen best leaders in a city or state who are not serving in government and presenting them with a special opportunity to apply their leadership talents to their highest and best use. The program consists of four stages.

Stage 1 is called "Exploring." Skeptical private sector leaders get a chance to "hang out" with the governor for lunch on a quarterly basis to talk candidly about what government is really like. They can decide whether doing a stint in government is right for them. This stage might last several years.

Stage 2 is called "Developing." To advance to this stage, leaders go through a four-hour "Who interview" to determine whether they have the "skill and will" to perform well during the two-year Leadership Service Term. If so, they will sign the Leadocracy Pledge. They create a customized development plan. And they embark on executing it.

A typical development plan might include shadowing the head of an area in government the leader is considering. It might include getting an active government leader to serve as a mentor. It might include earning a one-year master's in public administration. And this stage concludes with the completion of a "strategy study" of the area that the leader seeks to run. The idea is to give the leader a chance to prepare to hit the ground running.

Stage 3 is called "Deploying." This is the "doing" part of the program. It is the two-year Leadership Service Term in government, which the leader completes before their seventieth birthday. We picked this target age because it would be when the leader is at the top of his or her capability arc. The leader will still have time to fall in love with government before approaching retirement age. Once deployed into a leadership role, some leaders may decide to serve longer than two years. Some may decide to leave government service after their two-year term is up. Regardless, I hope that these folks will find their government service to be the most enjoyable stage of their careers because of the chance to apply their leadership skills, learn some new ones, achieve meaningful results, and meet interesting people.

Stage 4 is called "Mentoring." Leaders who have completed their Leadership Service Term will be available as mentors to people who are in the earlier stages of the program.

The Future Vision

I am incredibly excited about The Leaders Initiative. By the time this book hits shelves, the first TLI chapter will be up and running in Colorado, thanks to the support and vision of Governor Hickenlooper. When I asked the governor if I could count on him to help me recruit the initial TLI group, and to "hang out" with them at lunch quarterly, he replied, "Yes! It's a no-brainer." He understands better than most how crucial great leadership is. As we move forward, we'll be measuring the performance of the members and the satisfaction of everybody involved. If this pilot in Colorado isn't a success, we'll redesign the model and try again. If it is a success, we will start replicating TLI chapters in other states and local communities. Then we'll go to the national level. Then we will go international.

Already, great minds are contributing ideas for how to make the organization successful and the experience for members positive. Mark Gallogly suggested that we work to align our training with future leadership needs in communities. "Think about proactively planning for future needs in government and use the scorecard approach to recruit, retain, and develop dedicated and gifted people over time."

Professor Csikszentmihalyi recommended something similar. "What I would ask governors to do is create a task force that evaluates agencies or departments for how a position could be created for a private sector person to fill there. In other words, prepare the nest before you lay the egg. Then you could give the members many options. Or develop a template for recognizing the challenges for each agency. Identify some major problem that needs to be solved and for which either there is no one prepared to do it or it's not well enough covered." Align challenges in government with the skills of the members, he was telling me. This is how TLI would help people achieve flow.

We have a big goal for TLI: that fifteen hundred of

society's greatest leaders complete their leadership service term by 2030.

Imagine the dramatic global improvement in the quality of life that would occur if fifteen hundred of society's greatest leaders got into government. I believe it would be significant, and visible to the naked eye.

We want the idea of The Leaders Initiative to spread everywhere. Improving the quality of leadership in every country makes all of our lives better. Safe and stable societies improve freedom and opportunity and prosperity for their citizens. And free, thriving, and prosperous citizens are more likely to peacefully trade with one another. Whereas bureaucracy leads to waste and conflict, I believe leadocracy will lead to a higher quality of life and greater peace among nations.

Sign the Leadocracy Pledge

When authors write about what others *ought* to do but do not do so themselves, it makes their messages less credible. But when authors write about something they believe in and then do something about it, I find myself extra-inspired to take action. So I have chosen take action now, to try to lead by example, and to inspire you to take action, too.

I've signed the Leadocracy Pledge. I'm committing to doing a stint in the government. And that scares me. It's a commitment that I wasn't willing to make until very recently.

What changed? Through the process of writing this book and starting The Leaders Initiative, I've learned a few things. First, there is an urgent need for leadership in government. Second, you *can* actually make a difference in government—the situation is not hopeless. Third, I have a real desire to make an impact in this way, to work toward bettering my community

The Leadocracy Pledge

Be the change that you want to see in the world.
—Gandhi

I, __Geoff Smart__ ,
will complete a full-time, two-year leadership role in
government by my seventieth birthday.

_G SS_
Signature

_12/1/2011_
Date

Make the Leadocracy Pledge at www.leadocracy.org

The Leadocracy Pledge

Be the change that you want to see in the world.
—Gandhi

I, _____ ,
will complete a full-time, two-year leadership role in
government by my seventieth birthday.

_____
Signature

_____
Date

Make the Leadocracy Pledge at www.leadocracy.org

as a small but exciting portion of my career. And fourth, if you work with the right elected leader, it can be a fun leadership adventure of a lifetime.

I'm thirty-nine years old as I write this, so I have three decades to honor this commitment. It's somewhat comforting to have that kind of time. Still, it is kind of scary—but definitely exhilarating. I'm thinking about it now, and planning for it. For example, I plan to continue to volunteer as leadership advisor to my governor and to other leaders at the national, state, and local levels. I plan to give speeches on leadocracy and consult with heads of state around the world. When our kids have left us empty-nesters, my wife and I might go back to school. In my late forties or early fifties, I have my eye on doing Harvard's one-year Mid-Career Master in Public Administration in the Kennedy School of Government. I have heard great things about that program. In my mid-fifties is when I will get serious about choosing the specific job in government, with the specific set of leadership problems I could be most helpful in solving. If I perform well, and if I like it, I might do another stint, or return to private life and resume volunteering my time and energy to advance this movement and other causes I care about.

• • •

The Leaders Initiative has the potential to be a catalyst in the leadocracy movement. I encourage you to create and implement a solution like it, or different from it. It is not the only solution. But it is a solution that I believe will help push aside the curtain of mystery standing between our greatest leaders and government service.

We need more great leaders in government. If you know someone who fits the bill, spread the word. Tell them about The Leaders Initiative. Buy them a copy of the book. And urge them to sign the Leadocracy Pledge.

The Leadocracy Discussion

1. What do you think of the design of The Leaders Initiative? How would you improve it, to make it easier for great leaders in the private sector to ease into government?
2. Do you know anyone whom you would love to see sign the Leadocracy Pledge?
3. If you are a great leader, what would it take for *you* to sign the Leadocracy Pledge or start or join a TLI chapter in your city?

CHAPTER 8

Living in a Leadocracy

Effective leadership is not about making speeches or being liked;
leadership is defined by results not attributes.
—*Peter Drucker*

What would it feel like to live in a leadocracy?

The short answer is, it would feel awesome.

Things would just . . . work.

Consider the differences between a well-managed hotel and a poorly managed hotel. In the great hotel, you are greeted with a smile. The TV remote control works. The pillows are comfortable. There is complimentary toothpaste waiting for you in the bathroom (since yours was likely swiped at airport security). When you have a problem, you call the front desk and it is resolved promptly and courteously. Doesn't that sound better than being greeted by a surly front-desk attendant who ignores you, not being able to watch TV, having a lousy night's sleep, or having bad breath for your meeting in the morning?

A leadocracy will not be all roses and rainbows. Life will still have human struggle. Bad people will still do bad things. There will still be broken hearts and unfulfilled dreams.

But government would no longer be a source of constant angst. Government would be a source of safety and stability.

When I set out to discover more about government, I was expecting to find that it is impossible for even great leaders to make a difference—that the growing bureaucracy has frozen all progress. But instead I found many examples of great leaders making a difference, making communities significantly better.

And the phenomenon of great leaders from the private sector going into government is not unheard of. It's just rare. I would love to see this phenomenon amplified—to twist the dial all the way up.

What would that look like—if most or all government leadership positions were filled by the greatest leaders in our society? I think for the average citizen, for all of us, the positive effect of leadocracy on quality of life would be visible to the naked eye. Why? Because we would have (1) greater safety, (2) greater freedom, and (3) greater opportunity.

Greater Safety

Citizens generally do not seem to want a bumbling and micromanaging government that is heavily involved in their lives. I don't. Citizens want government to provide a safe and stable platform on which to live their lives.

Citizens want well-paved and clean streets on which to drive to work. They want a feeling of security leaving a movie theater in an urban neighborhood late at night. They want more effective management of services to help society's most vulnerable citizens—abused children, chronically homeless people, special-needs people. They want clean air and drinking water.

And they want the financial safety that comes from balanced budgets and avoiding huge government debt. Mitch Daniels recognized this need in Indiana's citizens when he

What would that look like—if most or all government leadership positions were filled by the greatest leaders in our society?

I think for the average citizen, for all of us, the positive effect of leadocracy on quality of life would be visible to the naked eye.

took office as governor. He had a focus on getting Indiana out of a severe budget crisis, which meant reducing the state employee payroll. Yet despite fewer employees, most agencies have vastly improved services. The Department of Human Services and others have won national awards.

Even with the necessary belt-tightening, Governor Daniels also knew that he needed to prioritize the safety of citizens and the safety of children. He worked to increase the number of state police by about four hundred troopers, a 45 percent increase. And to improve the welfare of Indiana's at-risk children, he worked to add more than *eight hundred* caseworkers in the Department of Child Services.

Earl Goode, Governor Daniels's chief of staff, told me about these changes. "We're doing more with less in almost every agency," he said. "But in some areas, we had to add people to do the job right." And they were able to do so because of the careful financial management of all other agencies and the appropriate allocation of the resources of the state.

When he was mayor of Denver, John Hickenlooper discovered the incredible cost of homelessness for the city, from both a financial and humanitarian perspective. So he started Denver's Road Home in partnership with Mile High United Way. After five years in operation, the organization had decreased the chronic homeless population by more than 60 percent by providing housing. It had decreased panhandling in key areas by 83 percent. It had raised more than $46 million to support various initiatives. It had provided a vast array of services to prevent thousands of people from becoming homeless. It won awards from the U.S. Department of Housing and Urban Development and other organizations. That is awesome.

And the cost to the city of providing services to homeless

people went from about $40,000 per person served to about $16,000 per person.

To have a greater quality of life, we have to have greater safety. And it is possible to make that happen without bankrupting our communities.

Greater Freedom

Citizens want the freedom to make choices that optimize their enjoyment of life. They don't like it when government gets in the way of that.

They want freedom to start innovative businesses, freedom from excessive red tape. They want freedom to earn income and exchange goods and services, freedom from an excessive tax burden. They want freedom from bureaucracy that limits their enjoyment of life, liberty, and the pursuit of happiness.

Imagine your last trip to your state's department of motor vehicles. You may have been lucky if it was painless. Most of us dread not just interactions with the DMV, but interactions with almost any government office. Earl Goode described efforts in Indiana to make interactions with government as painless as possible. Some of the most obvious improvements occurred in the Bureau of Motor Vehicles.

"They told us you could never get the transaction time in the Bureau of Motor Vehicles below thirty minutes. The transaction is when you actually start what you came in to do." Who came up with this number? A government-efficiency group that Governor Daniels created when he took office. It worked with all the agencies on identifying opportunities for improving the state operation. "Right now, we have 1,350 fewer employees in the BMV. The average transaction time, across the whole state, is *less than eight minutes*. From when you walk in the door to when you leave, it's about sixteen minutes."

Amazing! Even the efficiency experts didn't think it was possible, but the leaders were able to make it happen. They gave the employees tools. They gave them better technology. They made it possible to do more through the BMV website. And they gave branch managers incentive bonuses. Earl told us proudly, "The BMV was the first agency, state or federal, to win the customer excellence in customer quality for two years in a row."

To make government run more efficiently and effectively requires freeing resources from inefficient sinkholes. Fred Steingraber was able to do that and refocus resources toward the priorities of Kenilworth's citizens. "We have street sweeping in our community. I found out before I was elected that the street sweeping machine was going to have to be replaced. It would have been a $200,000 investment. When I became president I said, we aren't going to do that. Certainly, clean streets were important to citizens. But $200,000 for a piece of equipment we used less than ten times per year?" Fred knew he could find a more cost-effective way. The solution was outsourcing. Fred contacted nearby communities and negotiated a deal for one of them to handle Kenilworth's street cleaning. "It is now costing us about $7,000 a year and we are getting better service and don't have investment and on-going maintenance and repair costs."

And when he found out that the village tax district was paying the park district (a separate local tax district) to handle park lawn maintenance for both the village and park districts? He told the village manager to contact local landscaping companies to find out what it would cost to outsource the lawn maintenance for both districts. This resulted in a 75 percent cost savings and a redeployment of personnel from the park district to higher-value-added work, serving both tax districts. He has continued down this path, and the village has secured multiple collaborative community agreements, resulting in savings for materials, services, and even infrastructure. Finally, he has worked with three communities to undertake a shared governance business model for their emergency 911 dispatch services, which will result in savings, lower investment per community for new technology, and enhanced emergency and catastrophic support service.

By carefully analyzing, efficiently allocating, and aligning teams, these great leaders have increased government efficiency and freed citizens from excessive bureaucracy and tax burdens.

Greater Opportunity

Citizens want the opportunity to improve themselves, to be all that they can be. Having a safe and stable government, focused on freedom for citizens, means that more opportunities will start to pop like popcorn, for all citizens.

Citizens want the opportunity to have a job that fits their talents and interests. They want the opportunity to get a high-quality education, for themselves and their children. They want the opportunity to spend more time helping other people rather than spending all of their time just trying to stay afloat. These things require a thriving economy to provide job opportunities and tax revenue to support government services.

All of the governors with private sector experience that I spoke with were laser-focused on improving the strength of their economies and the success of businesses in their states. Governor Jack Markell is bringing about educational reform in Delaware. Other than the obvious benefits to future generations of children, an added benefit is making Delaware more attractive to businesses, and that means jobs. A better-educated populace means a stronger workforce. But he did not stop there. Governor Markell wanted to become BFFs with existing and potential employers. No, not best friends forever.

BFF stands for "business finder's fee"—a tax credit bonus that tax payers get if they refer a business that brings jobs to his state. How cool is that? Governor Markell also said that he is the first governor to implement Salesforce.com to track progress in key metrics related to economic development.

Governor Hickenlooper's new head of economic development, Ken Lund, is on a tear, too. The duo recently attracted Arrow Electronics to Colorado from New York City, which will bring thousands of jobs to the state. This is the ninth Fortune 500 company to relocate to Colorado. This is not an accident. The governor has created a giant "blueprint" (like a scorecard for job creation) that includes measurable outcomes under these important priority areas: "Build a Business-Friendly Environment," "Retain, Grow, and Recruit Companies," "Create and Market a Stronger Colorado Brand," "Educate and Train the Workforce of Tomorrow," "Cultivate Innovation and Technology."

"I've always said that we'll move at the speed of business, not the speed of government," Mitch Daniels told me. "We've organized our whole administration around the objective of building a better economic climate. And the first step we took was to abolish this state bureaucracy called the department of commerce, which hadn't really generated any commerce that I could find, and replace it with what we thought would be a better system, which has since been copied in a number of other states. It is a nonprofit corporation called the Economic Development Corporation that gets public funding but also raises private money. It can move quickly. A thousand-plus transactions later and I've been told over and over by the businesses that come here, 'Your team, it's like talking to businesspeople, not government bureaucrats.' It has made a huge difference."

"Our role is a customer service business," Governor Rick

Snyder said. "And our customers are the citizens in our state and the organizations in our state. Our role is to be an enabler to create a playing field for free enterprise to work and for people to have a great quality of life and success. We're providing the environment of success."

A prime application of this philosophy is Governor Snyder's approach to growing commerce, jobs, and the economy in Michigan. "It's the concept of hunting versus gardening," he said. "What you find quite often is that states use incentives to essentially buy businesses into their state. And that would be known as hunting. You're going out of state, out of country in some cases, to attract businesses. Gardening is the concept of looking to entrepreneurs or existing companies in your state and helping them grow. If you do the database analysis, you'll find most jobs come from businesses already in your state growing and flourishing. We had too much of a bias in the state toward hunting, so I've reversed that. Business 101 states that you always take care of your current customers before you go after new customers. Once you're doing gardening well and you're starting to hunt, what's the very best marketing to use? It's not incentives, it's not the trade commission, it's not TV ads. It's great word of mouth from happy customers."

• • •

I can see two futures.

The first future is one in which not many of our greatest leaders serve in government. In this future, in the hands of non-leaders, we suffer from increasing deficits and debts. Companies become so distrustful of government that they relocate to more stable and secure places (taking jobs with them). Dollars are allocated toward pet projects or cronies. There is no accountability or follow-through. Infrastructure starts to break down from lack of maintenance. Cities and towns start to smell and look bad. Citizens feel the situation growing increasingly desperate and they take to the streets to protest government incompetence and waste, but it makes no difference. On a daily basis, citizens face fear, burdens, fewer opportunities, and a quality of life that gets worse and worse.

There is another future.

The other future is leadocracy. It is a future in which society's greatest leaders serve in government. Men and women of truly exceptional leadership ability and character.

In this future, in the hands of great leaders, our society becomes increasingly safe and stable. Debts get paid off and budgets are balanced. Innovators innovate. Workers work.

Dollars are allocated towards the society's highest priorities and are managed in a way that minimizes waste and maximizes the value of the results. Stuff works.

Government is almost invisible in the daily lives of its citizens. Citizens take to the streets not to protest or to commit crimes, but to walk their kids to school, to go to work, and visit with friends. Everyone's quality of life improves.

I really don't feel like I'm alone in wanting this future. Citizens will decide to elect great leaders, and will build their capability to do so. Great leaders will get into government, and will apply their talent for the good of us all.

And the results will be awesome.

I believe that one day, I will hold my newborn grandson or granddaughter in the air. I will smile and say, "Life just gets better and better."

And it will be true.

Appendices

Q&A

1. *What does leadocracy mean?*
It means "government by society's greatest leaders."

2. *What's the big idea here?*
The big idea is that we are on a path of increasing bureaucracy, which is bad for everyone's quality of life.

However, there is a solution that will improve everyone's quality of life. "Hiring more great leaders into government" is the central solution that is proposed in this book.

3. *So you are saying every government leader should come from the private sector?*
No. The goal is more great leaders in government. I would be pleased if there were a mix of them who grew up in a variety of backgrounds—the public sector, the military, science, education, etc. But the main thrust of this book is driven by the realization that there are so many great leaders in the private sector, I would like to find ways to get more of that population into government. It is the largest untapped pool from which to draw great leaders.

4. Isn't this idea elitist?

No, I do not find it elitist. Elitist to me refers to something that is restricted to a subset of the population, ordained from birth. I believe that anybody can become a great leader. That is regardless of birth, color, religion, gender, sexual orientation, etc. I guess there are some exceptions, like a person in a permanent coma is not able to become a great leader. But generally, leadership is a skill that anybody can develop. It is the people who choose to invest the countless hours and blood, sweat, and tears into developing and honing their leadership skills whom I want leading my government.

5. But aren't all businesspeople dishonest, selfish, and corrupt? Just look at Enron, Madoff, and the rest. Why would we want more of them in government?

There are dishonest, selfish, and corrupt people from all backgrounds. Not all businesspeople are this way. I want the honest, generous, non-corrupt ones to serve in government.

6. Don't you realize that government is not the same thing as business?

Yes. However, I believe that the leadership skills that great private sector leaders develop, combined with the right temperament (e.g., flexibility, a spirit of generosity), can make for an exceptionally good public sector leader.

7. What qualifies you to write this book?

Not much, if you think government reform is all about laws. But if you think government reform is all about leadership, then you may find my background and perspective relevant. I admittedly do not have formal training in constitutional law, and I have not spent decades testing these ideas in a government setting. However, my training and experience as a leader and studier of leaders, combined with some amazing recent experiences in government and my interviews with government leaders over a year, led me to feel comfortable that the ideas in this book have value and should be communicated.

8. *Why did you write this book?*
My life's mission statement is "to enjoy life and help others enjoy theirs." My professional mission statement is "to create, communicate, and put into practice useful ideas about leadership."

The opportunity to apply hiring practices from the private sector to government advances both of these missions.

And doing this book project was fun. Writing this was not at all a chore. It was a joy to work with the governors and interview people who had made the leap from the private sector into public sector. I am thrilled to share their stories.

• • •

I really appreciate your reading this book. I hope that if you found its message useful, you help to spread the word. Thank you.

ACTION
For Voters
Vote smart!

Find downloadable tools like the Leadocracy Scorecard and watch short videos by Geoff Smart at www.leadocracy.org.

Please buy copies of *Leadocracy* and give them to your friends and coworkers who are interested in improving their quality of life.

For Government Leaders

Hire smart! Read *Who: The A Method for Hiring* to improve your hiring success of key cabinet and staff members.

Buy copies of *Leadocracy*, give them to your staff and say, "We are implementing this."

Find downloadable tools like the Leader Accomplishment Record and watch short videos by Geoff Smart on how to put leadocracy principles into practice at www.leadocracy.org.

Are you a head of state? Would you like to achieve better results through leadocracy? If so, contact Geoff.Smart@ leadocracy.org to schedule a phone consultation or a visit with Geoff Smart.

For Private Sector Leaders

Are you a successful private sector leader? Find hints about how to do a stint in government here www.leadocracy.org.

Are you considered one of the fifteen best leaders in your state? Are you interested in testing your leadership skills, learning new skills, and applying your talents toward achieving challenging and meaningful outcomes? If so, please contact Geoff.Smart@leadocracy.org for guidance, or go here to learn more about how to start a chapter of The Leaders Initiative in your area: www.theleadersinitiative.org.

Acknowledgments
of Awesomeness

There were many generous people who contributed to this book. Here is the cast of characters, in chronological order.

I dedicated this book to my father, Brad Smart, who encouraged discussions around the dinner table about social issues of the day. And he taught me a lot about evaluating leaders and sparked my interest in the field of leadership. Peter Drucker was a mentor in graduate school. Learning about management from the "father of management" was as special as learning philosophy at the knee of Socrates. Marshall Goldsmith has been my book-publishing mentor, for which I am deeply appreciative.

Four people directly inspired the creation of this book. Mark Gallogly is a business leader who spends significant time influencing government reform at the national level; it was his suggestion to consider rounding up like-minded private sector leaders and grooming them for future government leadership roles. Blair Richardson sent me the email asking me to provide leadership advice to our new governor to help him hire his cabinet. And last but not least, Governor John Hickenlooper and his profoundly talented chief of staff, Roxane White, and their cabinet leaders were the ones who showed me that private sector leaders *can* make a big positive impact on government and the functioning of a society.

The education reformers Wendy Kopp (Founder of Teach For America) and KIPP Founders Mike Feinberg and Dave Levin provided support, guidance, and encouragement to write the book and start TLI. More than your words, your example is a profound motivation for us all.

The founding executive director of The Leaders Initiative, Josh Rubenstein, has contributed clarity of thought and passion for this daunting and worthy mission to structure and scale this organization. Retired U.S. Navy Admiral Ray Smith (former top leader in charge of the Navy SEALs) gave useful feedback about making the central message of this book an "and" message, not an "or" message. We need great leaders from all sectors to serve in government, and this includes encouraging more private sector leaders who are currently on the sidelines to get in the game.

A big thanks to the other governors, staff, and thought leaders who shared their stories of private-sector-to-public-sector leadership.

My editor Lari Bishop and the entire Greenleaf Book Group publishing team treated this project with the highest degree of professionalism. Clint Greenleaf, its CEO, treated me to delicious Texas barbecue, hired and deployed a highly talented team, and let them do their job—great job Chris McRay, Aaron Hierholzer, and Jenn McMurray. The publicity team knocked my socks off, led by Barbara Henricks, Jessica Kracoski, and Rusty Shelton. And the book marketing strategists Kevin Small and Mat Miller provided great perspective, expertise, and follow-through. My research collaborator, University of Chicago Professor Steve Kaplan, and his RA, Robert

Meyer, ran the statistics on CEO interest in government. And my ghSMART colleagues, like *Who* coauthor Randy Street and our *The Ideal Leader* coauthor Alan Foster, were kind enough to let me morph our methods to fit the public sector environment, and to allow me to give you an early peek at our work that is coming down the pipe. Thanks also for running our firm as president so capably, Randy, so I can invest time in do-gooding activities like this one. Linda Naden managed the impossible—arranging the interviews with governors, billionaire entrepreneurs, and other hard-to-reach folks—with her typical grace and charm. Ron Zoibi effectively managed all of the financial, regulatory, and IT-related tasks associated with this book project and oversaw the creation of the not-for-profit entity, The Leaders Initiative, to which all of the author royalties of this book are donated.

Thanks finally to my wife, Leslie, who is awesome on many levels, and whose limitless thinking and "go for it" spirit made taking on this book project feel less daunting. I appreciate her edits to improve this manuscript. I thank my kids. They are too young to understand much about the content of this book; however, it is the concern for their future world that partly motivated this project. One day I hope to be able to hold *their* kids in my hands and tell them that life just gets better and better. And it will.

Finally, thank you, for reading this book and for spreading the word of leadocracy.

Notes

1   Jeffrey M. Jones, "Americans Most Confident in Military, Least in Congress," June 23, 2011, Gallup.com http://www.gallup.com/poll/148163/Americans-Confident-Military-Least-Congress.aspx.

2   Steve Holland, "Most Americans Say U.S. on Wrong Track: Poll" (Reuters/Ipsos poll), Reuters, August 10, 2011. Kevin Hechtkopf, "Poll: Most Think U.S. on Wrong Track as Fears About Economy Grow" (CBS/*New York Times* poll), CBS News (online), September 16, 2011. Naftali Bendavid, "Country Is Headed in the Wrong Direction, 74% Say" (NBC/*Wall Street Journal* poll), *Wall Street Journal* (online), October 13, 2011.

3   Thomas Jefferson to Samuel Kercheval, July 12, 1816. From *Thomas Jefferson: Writings*, Merrill D. Peterson, ed., (New York: Library of America, 1984), 1395–1403; as quoted in *Thomas Jefferson* by Richard Bernstein (New York: Oxford University Press, 2003).

4   Estimates for the workforce based on the 2010 Occupational Employment and Wages survey, http://bls.gov/oes/. Numbers pulled for the "chief executive" and "general and operations managers" occupations, which the Bureau of Labor Statistics considers to represent top executive positions (see The Occupational Outlook Handbook, 2010-11 Edition, discussion of Top Executives, www.bls.gov/oco/ocos012.htm). Officer estimates based on the numbers of noncommissioned officers of rank E-7 through E-9 and commissioned officers of the rank captain or above for May of 2010 (U.S. Department of Defense, Personnel and Procurement Statistics, http://siadapp.dmdc.osd.mil/).

5   Michael Bloomberg, *Charlie Rose* (interview), PBS, September 12, 2011, www.charlierose.com/view/interview/11884.

6   Tim Hoover, "Hickenlooper Pursues Big Changes in Colorado Hiring, Firing," *The Denver Post* (online), November 4, 2011.

7   Mihaly Csikszentmihalyi, *Flow*, Harper Perennial Modern Classics, 2008 (originally published in 1990 by Harper & Row), 4.

8   Ibid, 3.

9   Ibid, 39.

10 Ibid, 42.

11 Michael Bloomberg, *Charlie Rose* (interview), PBS, September 12, 2011, www.charlierose.com/view/interview/11884.

About the Author

Geoff Smart is a CEO, bestselling author, and social entrepreneur whose mission is to create, communicate, and put into practice useful ideas about leadership.

Geoff serves as chairman and CEO of ghSMART. ghSMART is a leadership firm for CEOs and investors, which Geoff founded in 1995. The firm was named one of the "world's top firms" in Broderick's *The Art of Managing Professional Services*, and is the subject of two Harvard Business School cases titled "ghSMART & Co.: Pioneering in Professional Services."

Geoff is coauthor, with his colleague Randy Street, of the *New York Times* bestselling book *Who: The A Method for Hiring*. The book is one of the bestselling and most-acclaimed books in the world on the topic of hiring leaders, which *The Wall Street Journal* calls "the most important aspect of business." Soundview Executive Book Summaries gave *Who* the "Best 30 Business Books Award." *Shanghai Daily* named it a "Top 5 Best Business Book in China." Canada's *Globe and Mail* named *Who* the "#1 Best Business and Management Book of 2009." Geoff is also co-creator of the Topgrading philosophy of talent management.

As a social entrepreneur, Geoff is chairman and cofounder of SMARTKids Leadership Program, a 501(c)

(3) not-for-profit foundation. It provides a customized program of ten years of leadership mentoring and a $100,000 scholarship to top students with leadership potential from low-income communities. He is chairman and founder of The Leaders Initiative, whose mission is to elevate humanity by identifying, developing, and deploying society's greatest leaders into government. Geoff and his ghSMART colleagues also provide pro bono leadership advisory services to leaders in the fields of education, healthcare, and government.

Geoff earned a B.A. in economics with Honors from Northwestern University, and an M.A. and Ph.D. in psychology with emphasis in leadership from Claremont Graduate University, where he was a student of Peter F. Drucker. He was elected to Sigma Xi, the honorary society for holders of doctoral degrees, and is a member of Young Presidents' Organization (YPO).

www.geoffsmart.com